The **NO-NONSENSE GUIDE** to

CONFLICT
AND PEACE

**Helen Ware (Ed), Peter Greener, Deanna Iribarnegaray,
Bert Jenkins, Sabina Lautensach, Jonathan Makuwira,
Dylan Matthews and Rebecca Spence**

The No-Nonsense Guide to Conflict and Peace
First published in the UK in 2006 by
New Internationalist™ Publications Ltd
Oxford OX4 1BW, UK
www.newint.org
New Internationalist is a registered trade mark.

Cover image: The Separation Wall in the West Bank. Marco Garofalo/G/N/
Camera Press.

Series editor: Troth Wells
Design by New Internationalist Publications Ltd.

 Printed on recycled paper by T J International Ltd, Padstow, Cornwall, UK
who hold environmental accreditation ISO 14001.

British Library Cataloguing-in-Publication Data.
A catalogue record for this book is available from the British Library.

Library of Congress Cataloguing-in-Publication Data.
A catalogue for this book is available from the Library of Congress.

ISBN: 978-1904456-421

The **NO-NONSENSE GUIDE** to
CONFLICT AND PEACE

'Publishers have created lists of short books that discuss the questions that your average [electoral] candidate will only ever touch if armed with a slogan and a soundbite. Together [such books] hint at a resurgence of the grand educational tradition... Closest to the hot headline issues are *The No-Nonsense Guides*. These target those topics that a large army of voters care about, but that politicos evade. Arguments, figures and documents combine to prove that good journalism is far too important to be left to (most) journalists.'

Boyd Tonkin,
The Independent,
London

About the authors

Professor **Helen Ware** is Chair of International Agency Leadership (Peace Building) at the School of Professional Development in the University of New England (UNE), Australia. http://www.une.edu.au/ **Sabina Lautensach** studied first in Canada and has a PhD from University of Otago (NZ). She is currently a research fellow at the Asia Institute of the University of Auckland and editor of the Australasian Journal of Human Security. **Peter Greener** emigrated to New Zealand in 1983 from the UK. He is an experienced child, family and adult psychotherapist. His most recent publications include Push for Peace (ed), 2005. **Deanna Iribarnegaray** is currently completing a PhD at the UNE on the topic of 'understanding global terrorism'. **Bert Jenkins** completed his PhD in 1991 and now works at the UNE as a senior lecturer in Peace Studies. His main areas of interest are the intersections with environment, development and peace. **Jonathan Makuwira** is a lecturer in Peace Studies at the UNE where he obtained his PhD in International Development. Prior to his doctoral studies he worked for the Council for NGOs in Malawi (CONGOMA). **Dylan Matthews** is a researcher on conflict issues and author of War Prevention Works (2001). **Rebecca Spence** is senior lecturer in Peace Studies at the UNE. She has conducted research and consultancies in South Africa, Timor Leste, Bougainville, Australia, Northern Ireland and the Solomon Islands.

Other titles in the series

About the New Internationalist

The **New Internationalist** is an independent not-for-profit publishing co-operative. Our mission is to report on issues of global justice. We publish informative current affairs and popular reference titles, complemented by world food, photography and gift books as well as calendars, diaries, maps and posters – all with a global justice world view.

If you like this *No-Nonsense Guide* you'll also love the **New Internationalist** magazine. Each month it takes a different subject such as *Trade Justice*, *Nuclear Power* or *Iraq*, exploring and explaining the issues in a concise way; the magazine is full of photos, charts and graphs as well as music, film and book reviews, country profiles, interviews and news.

To find out more about the **New Internationalist**, visit our website at **www.newint.org**

Foreword

TIMOR LESTE (East Timor) is the world's newest nation, born out of 24 years of Timorese resistance and fighting for the restoration of international legality and independence. For decades, we were told by the international community that we could never attain nationhood and that our dreams were totally unrealistic. Today we are a nation facing new challenges of having to consolidate unity among Timorese, build up the state administrative apparatus, oversee the management of financial and natural resources, and build a cohesive society with a viable economic future.

From the Indonesian invasion of December 1975 to the successful Referendum for Independence in August 1999, we never stopped fighting for our right to freedom and self-determination. Over that time, one third of the population died from widespread bombing and consequent destruction of cultivated areas, and the military campaigns to annihilate FRETILIN [liberation movement] fighters. These killings by the Suharto regime had the complicity of many foreign governments, even Western democracies. Thus the occupying regime could not be made accountable. Even after the referendum, the Indonesian Government backed armed militias that terrorized and killed innocent civilians. No family in Timor Leste has remained untouched by the violence.

Over the years of fighting for our lives, our liberty and the survival of our culture, we have learnt about conflict. We learnt how to dislodge a vastly wealthier colonial power with a population two hundred times our own. We learnt how to keep our issue before a world of *realpolitik* that thought we were too small to count and dismissed our human rights in order to maintain good relations with Indonesia. We also learnt the evils of internal conflict in which brothers fight against brothers.

We learnt that national unity, international solidarity and the media are powerful means to mobilize support for our struggle. The worldwide broadcast of the Dili massacre of 12 November 1991 awakened ordinary people and shocked the world, including those who had provided the means for the Indonesian army's terror.

I myself had to live outside my homeland for 26 years (1973-1999). I joined the resistance in 1974, as a member of the first-ever FRETILIN Committee in exile, in Lisbon. In 1976, with help from the Campaign for the Independence of East Timor and Australian Trade Unions, I went to Australia to operate a mobile radio station to communicate with FRETILIN fighters in Timor Leste. This was illegal as the Australian Government prohibited any radio communication with the Timorese resistance. We had no other means of obtaining information on the Indonesian invasion and atrocities by their army. When the radio station was confiscated by the Australian police in September 1976, I was arrested and imprisoned. But the Darwin court released me. Then, forced to leave Australia, I went to Mozambique.

Throughout, we always strove to reach a common understanding among Timorese from many different political persuasions. Dialogue and respecting the opinions of others, within a well-established set of principles, have strengthened our national unity.

This experience of conflict in my own nation and my life makes it a great pleasure to write this Foreword to *The No-Nonsense Guide to Conflict and Peace*. Everyone will find in it ideas with which they agree and ideas which they would strenuously debate. But that is the point: conflict is not in itself evil – without conflict we, the Timorese, would have had great difficulty in gaining our independence so soon. What matters is how conflict is dealt with – and this is the theme of this highly worthwhile book.

Estanislau da Silva,
Minister for Agriculture, Forestry and Fisheries,
Timor Leste

CONTENTS

Introduction

In 1971, standing in a market in Eastern Nigeria, I commented how many vultures were settled on the roofs of the meat stalls. 'Ah,' said my companion, an ex-general from the Biafran army, 'isn't it wonderful to see them back? During the war they were all away on the battlefields.' Only people who have lived through war can truly appreciate peace. Nigeria showed me how pragmatically colleagues, who had fought on opposite sides, worked together to solve practical problems without rancor or recriminations, in a lasting peace which was greatly assisted by a booming economy. We hear so much about the enduring nature of inter-ethnic hatreds that it is salutary to realize that even civil wars do end and that people in Nigeria then, as in Cambodia or Mozambique now, do get back to planting their crops and raising their children if the politicians will let them.

What we learn as children about conflict, peace and justice stays with us for life – which is why it is so unfortunate that dealing with discord is a skill rarely taught in schools. And why it is especially tragic that children who have never learnt to play are taught to use guns for real.

I had two grandfathers: one jailed as a pacifist during the First World War and the other a patriotic volunteer for France who came back deeply shocked and totally opposed to the sheer random wastage of war. My parents were equally divided, since my mother was a pacifist medical researcher and my father developed new explosives.

The debates of my childhood as to how to deal with men who attack with guns are still valid today. However, two things have changed. Firstly, nine wars out of ten are now civil wars in which the great majority of the casualties are civilians. And secondly, we know much more about working to build peace and that there are techniques for conflict resolution which work.

As a diplomat in Zambia in the 1980s I dealt with exiled radicals from South Africa and Namibia, who were either freedom fighters or terrorists depending on one's viewpoint. When the leaders of the South African army first met with the armed wing of ANC, it was a revelation to see how the fighters shared so much more in common than the civilians. This was a great time to be where freedom was finally on the march, especially for the ordinary people who had suffered for so long.

Now I and my colleagues work as a team, teaching and researching peace studies at the University of New England in rural Australia. We are ethnically, religiously and ideologically a very mixed group from Australia, England, Malawi, Northern Ireland and Sri Lanka. Opinions range from the absolute pursuit of nonviolence to a pragmatic acceptance that faced with a Rwanda, a Kosovo or a Darfur, nonviolence cannot save lives fast enough. But we share a passion for peace and justice. This book is the product of our working together and our desire to share our knowledge of peace-building from the grassroots up.

Helen Ware
Armidale, Australia

1 War and peace

'After a lifetime of war-watching, I see war as an endemic human disease, and governments the carriers.'
Martha Gellhorn (1908-1998),
US journalist and author.

Conflict need not be a bad thing, but it can quickly spin out of control. With so much violence in the world we need to understand its causes and find ways to deal with it.

'VIOLENCE JUST HURTS those who are already hurt; instead of exposing the brutality of the oppressor, it justifies it,' noted Cesar Chavez, leader of the US United Farm Workers' union. Fights and upsets between people and groups are a part of everyday life, at home, at work, with family, friends or colleagues. They occur because each of us has needs, beliefs and desires and works towards fulfilling them as best we can. Tensions result when the goals and aspirations of one party clash with or contradict those of others.

Clashes occur at different levels and scales. First, there is personal conflict: 'Shall I be good (diet)? Or shall I be happy (chocolate)?' Second is disagreement between individuals: 'My football team is better than yours'/'No, mine is'. Thirdly, there is discord between distinct groups (communities, militant groups, government departments, non-governmental organizations (NGOs), corporations and agencies). Finally, there is international conflict that usually takes place between states or between coalitions of nations. As with the 'War on Terror', some of today's violence cuts across national borders and makes it difficult to see who is on 'our' side and who is on 'theirs', which makes life very difficult – for example for Muslims born or living in Western countries.

Many international conflicts in the post-Cold War

era take place within states and thus are civil or 'intra-national'. These are mostly based on distinctions of difference that occur within a nation – between different indigenous, ethnic, language and/or religious groups often opposing the dominant groups in the state.

Creative differences

Sometimes of course major differences can be creative and do not inevitably have to lead to violence. Like other social processes, the outcome is determined by the nature of the issues, the number of people involved and the relationships between them. How people respond to and manage differences will determine whether the outcome is violence or new, positive developments. For example, a film crew arguing with each other over artistic matters may create a confused disaster or a creative triumph. Conflict can prevent stagnation; stimulate interest and curiosity, the airing of problems, the development of solutions. External conflict can promote internal group cohesion. Creatively handled, discord can enable social structures to readjust by eliminating sources of dissatisfaction and removing the causes for opting out, so creating a new balance in a society.

There are many ways to 'manage' conflict: through accommodation, policy changes, legal processes, mediation and negotiation, as well as through the use of force. The possible outcomes include:

- A lose-lose situation where all parties are discontented with the outcome (all the fish are killed during the fighting).
- A win-lose situation where the needs of one (or more) party are met or perceived to have been met to a greater extent than for the other party(s) (one party gets most of the fish).
- A desirable win-win situation where needs of all parties are addressed to the satisfaction of all (a new, sustainable fishery development is equitably shared).

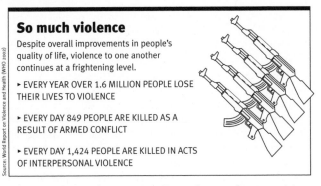

Source: World Report on Violence and Health (WHO 2002)

So much violence

Despite overall improvements in people's quality of life, violence to one another continues at a frightening level.

▸ EVERY YEAR OVER 1.6 MILLION PEOPLE LOSE THEIR LIVES TO VIOLENCE

▸ EVERY DAY 849 PEOPLE ARE KILLED AS A RESULT OF ARMED CONFLICT

▸ EVERY DAY 1,424 PEOPLE ARE KILLED IN ACTS OF INTERPERSONAL VIOLENCE

Are we inherently or naturally violent and competitive, or is this a learned response? (see box 'Programmed for violence?' in chapter 2). Whatever the answer, one of the most common causes of discord is disputes over access to and use of resources. The more scarce the resource, the greater the likelihood of tension. However, there is always scope for learning to compromise and co-operate rather than competing to 'win'. As seen, we mostly find ourselves at odds out of our desire to do everything necessary to secure our basic needs.

People may indeed be willing to fight for abstract rights, such as freedom of speech or the right to self-determination, before basic needs. In this case, there can only be resolution if these contingent needs are addressed directly.

There are many other reasons too. Discord can also arise from injustice, human rights abuses and inequality created by repressive social, cultural, structural and economic frameworks or socio-political systems. In this case, the settlement has to address the injustices and allow for changed systems to build fairer relationships and interactions that promote equity, justice and peace.

Destructive conflict tends to blow up because the harmful and dangerous elements overcome those

> 'You must have been taught – and I was taught – that peace is the opposite of war. But is it? In India, peace is a daily battle for food and shelter and dignity. Arundhati Roy (1961-), Indian writer and activist. ∎

people who would keep it within bounds. As the disagreement expands there is increasing reliance upon power, threats, coercion and deception, and movement away from persuasion, conciliation, minimization of differences and the enhancement of mutual understanding and goodwill. Within each of the conflicting parties there is increasing pressure for uniformity of opinion and a tendency for the leadership to be taken over by the more extreme groups who are better organized for combat. Escalation results from competition to win, misperceptions and uncritical commitment to the cause.[1] This is why early intervention works so much better.

Today's conflicts

Since the end of the Cold War in 1989, there has been a shift from international aggression to civil wars. Although there have been wars between states such as those fought by the 'coalitions of the willing' in Afghanistan and Iraq, conflicts within a country are more common today as seen in Aceh and West Papua (Indonesia), Bougainville (Melanesia), Chechnya in Russia, Israel/Palestine, Sierra Leone, Sudan, and Sri Lanka. Frequently, these internal conflicts are over issues such as justice, political representation, security and self-determination. Discontent may lead to demands for political change, a separate state, increased participation in decision-making and equality in relation to issues of race or identity recognition (of ethnic, religious or linguistic differences). A number of these conflicts arise from historical mistakes that over time have led to animosity, stereotyping, domination and suspicion – positions that are now difficult to shift. For example, the Sri Lankan conflict that began in 1983 and is now hovering on the fragile 2002 ceasefire could have been stifled at the outset by an agreement for political power-sharing between the ethnic groups, but that was before the build-up of discrimination against the Tamils and the creation of political parties based on ethnic exclusion.

'It is said that our indigenous ancestors, Mayas and Aztecs, made human sacrifices to their gods. It occurs to me to ask: How many humans have been sacrificed to the gods of Capital in the last five hundred years?' Rigoberta Menchú Tum (1959-), Guatemalan activist for indigenous rights, and Nobel Peace Prize winner, 1992. ■

Another spur to warfare is resources. Conflict such as that in the Democratic Republic of Congo (DRC) is fueled by greedy corporations, caring little for the people that their activities often damage. 'Corporations should ensure their activities support peace and respect for human rights in volatile areas such as north-eastern Congo, not work against them,' says Anneke Van Woudenberg of Human Rights Watch.

Violence
Unfortunately, violence is still the main means used in attempting to resolve conflict. This is as true for crime on the streets, violence in schools and in homes, as it is for the role of militants or the police and troops engaged in controlling civil disturbance or fighting wars in the interests of a state. Violence is just one method of pursuing social, economic and political goals. There are many alternatives (see final chapter) but where these appear to have failed, the situation often spins out to one of violence.

Civilians suffer most
Modern wars have a significant impact on civilians by destroying their homes and agricultural systems, polluting their water, land and air, and killing or injuring old people, women, children and parents.

There is also the catalogue of rape, torture, imprisonment, brutality, starvation, trauma and disease. Usually both sides have engaged in deplorable acts of terror. In the aftermath of such violence, societies are left angry and confused, seeking retribution and revenge to pay back perpetrators. In turn this feeds the cycle of violence, prolonging and perpetuating the fighting. This is why, sadly, the best statistical predictor of a civil war is an earlier civil war: conflicts are dampened down, simmer and then boil over again.

On the ground

Finding a resolution to conflict has to be approached from an all-round perspective where reflection on our own beliefs and analysis of the particular case are required to understand and evaluate each case. Yet there are remarkable similarities between strife in areas as distant from each other as Sri Lanka and

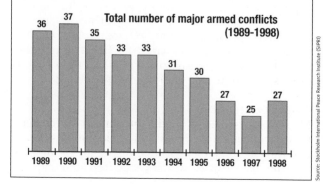

Up in arms

Apart from two rises in 1990 and 1998, the total number of armed conflicts has continuously declined since 1989. Those that emerged after 1989 have largely been successfully contained, in comparison with older continuing disputes. Only 5 of the 27 conflicts active in 1998 originated after 1989, which suggests that the longer and more intense these are, the harder it is to achieve peace. In 2003, the number was down to 19.

Total number of major armed conflicts (1989-1998)

1989: 36
1990: 37
1991: 35
1992: 33
1993: 33
1994: 31
1995: 30
1996: 27
1997: 25
1998: 27

Source: Stockholm International Peace Research Institute (SIPRI)

Northern Ireland. The same approaches used in international disputes can also be effective at the local level. This section considers the use of a few basic tools and processes to help bring peace.

Peacemakers from outside looking for ways to help people settle differences need to accept that they are effectively parachuting in to the situation. They bring with them their own cultural baggage as a product of socialization somewhere else. We naturally tend to read and interpret the world through our own personal, educational, social and cultural filters. Recognizing this is especially important when trying to end disputes in a different cultural setting. Everything we know and are sure of within our own society and culture may not be transferable. This leads to the challenges of sensitivity and 'co-learning' – a willingness to listen and learn from local people – before diving in, boots and all.

Every culture has its ways of dealing with discord. One of the first questions to ask is what these are. International intervention is inappropriate where, for example, the only obstacle is a lack of funds to allow local elders or others to travel around the country to meet together and calm the situation. Most societies have local people actively involved in peacemaking. It is important to find these people and ask what they are doing or would wish to do to promote peace. People everywhere seek survival and are not passive in the face of violence (although for minorities, such as the Papuans within Indonesia, lying low may be the only safe strategy because the Indonesian army has such power and impunity in mistreating them). Individuals organize activities in their communities to engage others in working to end the violence that is disrupting their lives. A dated colonial-style approach imposed from above makes such resolution difficult and is usually doomed to failure.

Effective peacemaking begins with the individual.

'World peace through nonviolent means is neither absurd nor unattainable. All other methods have failed. Thus we must begin anew. Nonviolence is a good starting point.' Martin Luther King (1929-1968), US civil rights activist, December 1964. ■

We all have to address conflict in our own communities rather than wait for a solution to materialize from outside. Since everyone has their own lens of experience through which they see the world, every person's perceptions of a conflict is different, even amongst those coming from the same locale. Sadly, the factors causing flare-ups are the same whether the spat is at a local, national or international level. They include the need to be right; the need to win at any cost; stereotypic views; the projection of biases; the tendency to allocate or transfer blame and to make decisions based mainly on economic rationalizations rather than on humanitarian grounds.

However, the same people who share these negative views can also become the main actors in any recovery process. Moving to peace is then a matter of shifting the balance towards the positive end of the spectrum; it involves a willingness to look beyond what might seem obvious, safe and the accepted norm and to think 'outside the box'. The bitterest conflicts often occur where there are no cross-cutting divides and ethnic, religious and class divisions all fall at the same points so that individuals will be discriminated against on all three grounds. Positive factors include co-operative bonds; group memberships across divides; common allegiances; religious or other values which are opposed to conflict; institutions, procedures and groups and an understanding of the costs of escalating violence.

The path to understanding
The first step in analyzing the dispute is to identify the key people, their issues and power relations as well as their previous actions. This information can

then be used to gain a deeper understanding about the background, motives and the factors that underpin the differences.[2] It is also important to pick out at least three distinct stages of a conflict and to differentiate between its visible and hidden aspects.[3] A method of 'mapping' can then explore the nature of the discord and examine possible underlying causes.[4] The map represents the main and peripheral parties and links them in different ways (using appropriate symbols) to depict the interactions between them.

Analysis and mapping are a practical means of engaging the parties to work together in a workshop setting with a facilitator. In this way they learn more about their own and others' different positions, perspectives and perceptions. The various groups each produce their own maps of the conflict from their own perspectives. The purpose is to give all involved an opportunity to be informed and have their views heard. This is crucial in order to negotiate a settlement based on their respective interests and separate needs rather than continuing to defend fixed positions. This offers mutual gains for all parties and gives greater chances of forging a path to reconciliation. Here, the conflict is the symptom and the aim is to diagnose and cure the ailment.

Another method, the 'appreciative inquiry' approach, provides a technique for dealing with strife as a way to find creative and positive solutions rather than as exercises in trying to solve a problem.[6] A further channel is 'constructive storytelling' in which people tell stories about the situation. This can be an effective means of building peace at the community level because stories are both accessible and inclusive.[7] Sometimes elements of conflict-mapping, aspects of appreciative inquiry and constructive storytelling (which are all good ideas despite their off-putting titles) can all be used. The key is that there is no 'one size fits all' approach.

Global conflict

At a global level, the dynamics of a conflict can be seen in terms of its history and motivating forces.[8] The three basic steps are:

1 Looking at the issues surrounding sovereignty.
2 Accepting the need for a multidisciplinary approach and involvement of different agencies.
3 Considering the importance or otherwise of working through the United Nations (UN) framework.[9]

Peacemaking

Reaching peace agreements built on genuine commitments to sharing power is often one of the main challenges. Third parties can play a vital role in finding a way through, whether in disputes between individuals or in international crises. Often their involvement can become the catalyst to build new relationships, restore trust and work towards reconciliation. They can help the mending of broken relationships even before agreements are signed and accords are drawn up, paving the way for a sustainable outcome based on work that deals with the root causes. Whether in workplace disputes or in peace talks – for example between the Government of Sri Lanka and the Liberation Tigers of Tamil Eelam (LTTE), mediated by the Norwegian Government – the third party is vital to listen and to give perspective and encouragement to both or all sides.

An advantage of outside mediation is that those battling can realize that there are options available that are more desirable than continuing to fight. Recognizing this is more difficult than it sounds, or the parties would have long since got to this point by themselves. Who is actually gaining from the continuation of fighting? Who stands to lose if peace broke out? These are key points to explore. In Papua New Guinea, for example, the key supporters of the '*raskol* gangs' who terrorize the capital at night include the private security firms who protect the more affluent citizens, leaving poor people once more to suffer. Equally, as the history of Prohibition in the US suggests, the greatest supporters of today's 'War on Drugs' are the drug barons who would suffer most if these drugs were legalized.

For third-party facilitation to work, a suitable environment is vital. All interested groups must be invited to and allowed to participate in the peacemaking process without being forced to do so. This is where timing can be vital. Negotiators talk of a conflict being 'ripe' for resolution when those fighting have reached a point of exhaustion, or lack resources, and can see the attractions of peace beginning to outweigh the reasons for continuing to fight. At this critical point, much may depend on those outside the country who are supporting the warring parties. In the Sri Lankan case, the fighting relied on funding by diaspora Sri Lankans who were not risking death in the conflict.

Mozambique: peace through mediation, trust and money

After 30 years of fighting, the final peace settlement in Mozambique (in 1992) was dependent on the thaw in the Cold War and the demise of apartheid in South Africa. But even though these changes secured the end of external financing, the civil war had built up such bitter divisions that peace seemed unattainable.

Only neutral and trusted civilians could bring together two sides that had refused to negotiate. It took the patient support, through 12 rounds of negotiations, by the Catholic lay community of St Egidio in Rome and the financing of backers including the Italian Government and the Lonrho companies, to ensure that peace was finally achieved and the UN could come in and supervise democratic elections. The people of the two sides in the war had certainly hated each other yet, little by little, they became compatriots. The lesson for other African civil wars could be that, given time and space, even the bitterest of enemies can achieve a workable political solution. ∎

In Mozambique the anti-Government RENAMO rebels were supported by an unlikely coalition of the then racist South African Government, US religious fundamentalists fighting 'Communism' and commercial freebooters with an interest in Mozambique's resources. Had the South African Government then had an interest in stopping the fighting at any point it could have done so. In fact the resolution came through the work of an Italian religious organization using 'second track' diplomacy (see box and also chapter 4).

In the DRC, the armies of neighboring countries have been heavily involved, both on behalf of their own governments but also just for their own benefit as looters of resources. In Uganda the Government agreed to the World Bank's demand to spend no more than two per cent of the national product on the military, but then went off to fight a war to plunder coltan (used in mobile phones) in the DRC to finance its army.

Changing cultures of violence

Moving from a culture of violence to one of peace requires concentrated efforts by all involved to transform the situation, rather than just to find an agreed solution on paper. As seen earlier, in the long term lasting peace cannot work until the underlying causes have been addressed. To make this happen, existing arrangements and behaviors that contribute to structural, cultural or ecological violence have to change: easier said than done. Although mediators play an important part in the first steps of transforming conflicts, it is the parties and their communities that must find the political and moral will to shift from war to peace.

Between nations and between warring groups alike, it is vital that ceasefires remain in place after agreements are signed to allow for peace-building to work.

Ideally, it should take no more than 12 months to move from the time a ceasefire is agreed and fighting stops to the point where peace-building is in full swing. This calls for good leadership, demobilization of the troops, security and a strong commitment to the process by everyone concerned in this unstable period.

The transition requires peacemakers to concentrate on renewing trust between the parties; building on their shared interests and achieving some successes together – whilst also ensuring that the fighting does not break out again.

Peace agreements and ceasefires are fragile. One spark can re-ignite the flame of conflict and take the whole process back to square one. Just one of the minor parties can create a climate of uncertainty in which the resumption of fighting is triggered, for example by a hostile rumor. A case in point was the 1994-1995 civil war in Ghana, known as 'the Guinea Fowl War' because the immediate cause was nothing more than a disagreement over the price of a bird in

---

Burundi: a perfect case for prevention

Rwanda's neighbor Burundi is effectively another holocaust in slow motion. The Tutsis – 14 per cent of the population – are accustomed to rule through their control over the army and bureaucracy. The 85 per cent Hutu population has long been discriminated against. Since the assassination of the first democratically elected and Hutu President Melchior Ndadaye by radical Tutsi soldiers in 1993, fighting has claimed 300,000 lives and displaced 1.3 million people out of a total population of 6.8 million. Sporadic attacks temporarily displace 25,000 to 50,000 residents each month. Some 800,000 Burundians live as refugees, mostly in Tanzania. The fiery situation is well known across the region and as a consequence external mediation by African presidents and former presidents, including Nelson Mandela, other countries, international organizations and NGOs tries to ensure that fighting does not boil over.

Lessons learnt so far in Burundi have been that:

1 Even with 15 political parties, everyone possible should be included in all talks. (Fortunately people all speak the national language Rundi).

2 Regional involvement is vital but not always effective.

the local market.

In such volatile circumstances, external intervention may be necessary to prevent violence flaring. Again, peacemakers have to work with the community to keep the peace and forge stronger relationships.[10]

Women fight for peace

Whilst women can be as aggressive as men, they play a greater role in peacemaking than in war-mongering. They can bring new elements into the peace process in many situations.[11] In Bougainville, for instance, women built community confidence in addressing 'restorative justice', which works not to punish the guilty but to respond to crime by repairing the harm done and restoring balance to the community affected. As Jossie Kauona Sirivi, of Bougainville Women for Peace and Freedom (BWPF) commented: 'Peace-building must also involve those alleged to have aided and abetted in the war.'

One of the challenges that they faced was helping

3 Significant numbers of Burundians see fighting as acceptable and do not consider the deaths of opponents to be of the same importance or moral weight as the deaths of fellow ethnic group members.

4 As in Rwanda, Christianity has a limited impact on curbing violence amongst its adherents (67 per cent of Burundians are Christians, 62 per cent of them Roman Catholics).

5 Idealistic NGOs working with children from both ethnic groups together (eg in 'football camps') have little impact if their parents stay opposed.

6 Life is exceptionally hard for couples in ethnically mixed marriages and their children.

7 No-one yet has succeeded in coming up with a win/win solution for both major ethnic groups (let alone the one per cent of Twa (Pygmies) who are routinely ignored).

8 The only real way of evaluating reconciliation and peace-building activities is by the continuance of peace. If fighting breaks out again they have clearly failed, whatever the textbooks or NGO reports say.

9 Experts are often misled into believing that what they want to happen (a reduction in ethnic divisions) is in fact happening. ∎

ex-combatants move back into society, including even those who had been involved in killing civilians in their own villages.[12] The women actually established a 'women only' village in the bush, so that they and their children could move away from abusive partners who had returned from the fighting in a disturbed state.

Psychological trauma is of course not limited to Western soldiers. In the Solomon Islands women banded together as mothers to go down to the barricades and talk to the young militia men and persuade them to come home. It is a measure of what normal life is like for women there that several female 'peace monitors' said that their lives had been improved by the civil violence because it had given them an opportunity for the very first time to have a say in how their communities are run. Whilst traditional and church leaders in the Solomons are male, the local peace-monitoring system, which was set up by an Australian-led regional peace-enforcing mission, had a strict gender equity provision for pairs of monitors: one female and one male to go around consulting with each village.

Books and reports about conflict often go rapidly out of date as claims of successful peacemaking are undermined by renewed violence. Burundi is a good example of a situation where only the bravest would claim success.[13] Good negotiators and mediators need to be optimists, but also realists.[14]

Seeds, soils and sweat

This is mediator John Paul Lederach's reply to a journalist who asked whether it was possible to talk about negotiation and peace with war still raging:

'I say hope is not negotiated. It is kept alive by people who understand the depth of suffering and know the cost of keeping a horizon of change as a possibility for their children and grandchildren. Quick fixes to long-standing violent conflicts are like growing a garden with no understanding of seeds, soils and sweat. This conflict traces across decades, even generations. It could take that long to sort it out.' ∎

---

1 M Deutsch *The Resolution of Conflict* (Yale University Press 1973) pp 351-2. **2** See www.ifm.eng.cam.ac.uk/dstools/choosing/confli.html **3** See www.intractableconflict.org/m/underlying_causes.jsp **4** See S Fisher et al 'Tools for conflict analysis' in *Working with Conflict* (Zed Books 2003) pp 17-35. **5** www.hawaii.edu/powerkills/WPP.CHAP10.HTM **6** The Appreciative Inquiry approach to conflict analysis is described by Rios and Fisher (2003), see note 4. **7** J Senehi 'Constructive Storytelling in Intercommunal Conflicts' in *Reconcilable Differences* (Kumarian Press 2000). **8** P Wallensteen 'Approaching conflict resolution' in *Understanding Conflict* (Sage 2002). **9** See A Morrison 'Disentangling disputes' in *Patterns of Conflict*, ed L Fisk and J Schellenberg (Broadview Press 2000). **10** J Rasmussen 'Negotiating a revolution – toward integrating relationship building and reconciliation into official peace negotiations' in *Reconciliation, Justice and Coexistence*, ed M Abu-Nimer (Lexington Books 2001). **11** S Anderlini 'The untapped resource – women in peace negotiations' in *Conflict Trends* (Accord/UNIFEM 2003). **12** R Soavana-Spriggs 'Bougainville women's role in conflict resolution' in *A Kind of Mending* (ANU Press 2003). **13** M Maundi 'Preventing conflict escalation in Burundi' in *From Promise to Practice* (International Peace Academy 2003) pp 345-346. **14** JP Lederach 'Cultivating peace: a practitioner's view' in *Contemporary Peacemaking*, eds J Darby and R MacGinty (Palgrave Macmillan 2003).

2 From divorce to war

In dealing with others, be gentle and kind.
In speech, be true.
In business, be competent.
In action, watch the timing.
No fight: no blame.
The Tao Te Ching

This chapter looks at what we can discover about resolving wars and civil disputes using the psychology of individual humans and from animal studies.

CLASHES, AS WE have seen, are not necessarily negative.[1] What is important is what we do with the crisis. Taken as an opportunity, conflict can create new openings or solutions not previously considered. Most importantly, finding ways to resolve differences between people can strengthen and deepen the relationship. That can allow the next blow-up to be dealt with swiftly and co-operatively. Here we explore conflicts: between people (inter-personal), between groups (inter-group), within countries (intra-national), and between nations (international) in order to look at their common elements.

As seen, sparring between individuals is usually among family, friends and colleagues. Between groups, disputes can occur between employers and employees; between professional groups; between interest groups and government, both national and local. All too often in today's world discord erupts between different religious, ethnic or racial groups. Even in Europe, when these conflicts cross the line from civil disobedience to outright fighting, they can spill over into civil war as happened in Northern Ireland in 1969.

In the post-Cold War world, conflicts raging

inside sovereign states have sadly become common: Somalia, Sierra Leone, Rwanda, DR Congo and the former Yugoslavia are some examples; also in Sri Lanka, Sudan and between Israelis and Palestinians. With the exception of the actions against Iraq, wars between nations are now rare, though attacks against rich world countries by Osama bin Laden's al-Qaeda terrorist network and its associates have brought a new awareness of conflict to millions around the globe who had previously felt secure.

Settling disputes

Negotiation, mediation and arbitration are the most common methods of settling disputes both between individuals and nations.

1 Negotiation

In negotiation, the most common method of handling international disputes, the two parties work together to resolve the difficulty between them.

2 Mediation

This introduces outside participation when those immediately involved are unable to negotiate a successful outcome between themselves. The mediator may do nothing more than provide the space for negotiations between the parties to continue. This has often been a role provided by the Secretary-General of the UN, providing his 'good offices' to the parties in a dispute. Some mediators are more active, suggesting potential solutions.

3 Arbitration

In arbitration, the authority to make a binding decision is vested in the arbitrator. The imposition of a decision can work, but arbitration often focuses on the legal aspects and does not consider the quality of the relationship between the parties. Arbitration can only work if the parties are prepared to move on without rancor once the decision has been implemented.

The best ex-President

For some, Jimmy Carter was not a very effective US President. Yet he still holds the distinction of being the only President since 1945 not to have ordered US troops into war. As an international mediator, he is arguably the best ex-President. His advantages are that everyone knows who he is and where he is coming from but no-one assumes that he represents current US policy. Carter does his homework including reading up on the psychological profiles of leaders he is going to speak to.

Carter's greatest success as a mediator was in Nicaragua in 1990 when, drawing on his own re-election failure in 1980, he was able to persuade the Sandinista President Daniel Ortega to accept his electoral defeat and step down peacefully.

Carter was also, at least for some time, a successful mediator in negotiations involving Haiti, Panama and North Korea. He has consistently opposed both US wars against Iraq. ■

Source: *Political Science Quarterly* Fall 1998.

The power of one

Personal conflict is concerned with one's perception of and responsibility for one's actions and the effect these have on the self and others. While such antagonisms usually involve two or more people, resolving the dispute takes only *one* person willing to take the first step toward a peaceful settlement – in Mahatma Gandhi's phrase: 'Whatever you do may seem insignificant, but it is most important that you do it.' But of course this is not the message we get from the media. Daily conflict can be as mundane as arguing over whose turn it is to take the children to school; bargaining over the price of a used car; or quarrelling with a neighbor over a barking dog.

Conflicts can be 'unilateral', 'bilateral', or 'multilateral'. A customer who simply refuses to pay a bill for no apparent reason puts the tradesperson who is owed the money into a unilateral conflict. A client who refuses to pay a plumber's bill because the drain is still not working creates a bilateral conflict for the plumber. Bilateral conflicts best describe a situation in which two parties want something from the other, or disagree over the process or the outcome of a particular situation. By contrast, a car accident involving a driver, a hitchhiker who gets hurt, and a pedestrian who was injured by the careless driver is a multilateral scenario.

The more parties involved in a dispute the more complicated and lengthy the settlement can be. A conflict can be defined by the number of people involved, and by its structure. 'Structural disputes' refers to the problems arising out of the situation rather than to the individuals involved. If trains are always late because of poor timetabling the fault lies with the timetable not the train drivers.

In addition, people's personalities play a part in the build-up and response to discord. Some examples are a) the attacker-defender; b) the accommodator; c) the avoider; and d) the stale-mater. Most people can easily see which category they themselves fit into, or sometimes watch themselves as they shift from one to the other. The debate continues as to how far there are gender differences in styles of conflict.[2]

It may appear obvious, but the desire to win can be blamed for the majority of serious conflicts. 'I want to buy your car – but only at the price I have decided on. You want to sell – but at twice my price.' This 'win-lose' approach, or 'zero-sum game' as it is often referred to in conflict literature, undercuts the need for compromise and co-operation. In a financial deal it is possible to 'split the difference' and arrive at a settlement.

Ideological or ethnic conflicts are often much harder to resolve precisely because neither side can contemplate 'splitting the difference'. One person can stop an argument from escalating into a conflict by refusing to be drawn into a win-lose situation. Proving others to be wrong is just another means to come out 'on top' and prevents successful outcomes. This attitude

The tree of conflict

This is a helpful image to use when talking with people involved in dispute. In groups, participants identify:

- The core problem behind the current conflict
- The principal root causes
- The main effects that have resulted from this problem

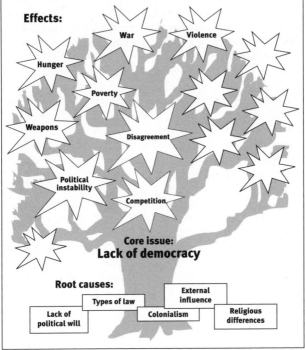

Effects:
War
Violence
Hunger
Poverty
Weapons
Disagreement
Political instability
Competition

Core issue:
Lack of democracy

Root causes:
Lack of political will
Types of law
Colonialism
External influence
Religious differences

stands in stark contrast to *ahimsa*, a concept that embraces nonviolence made famous by Gandhi during his struggle against British colonial rule in India. In its comprehensive meaning, *ahimsa* or non-injury teaches the avoidance of causing pain or harm either by thought, word, or deed.[3] This doctrine requires an attitude change from win-lose to win-win; from an antagonistic stance to one that finds middle ground.

You said it

In settling differences, the way people communicate is critical. Often we say things without thinking fully of the impact they have on the other person. Mis-communication can arise from a quarrel between people who do not share the same cultural or educational background, or the same language – or from the obvious assumption that two people should understand each other *because* they share the same language. During face-to-face negotiation, body language, facial expressions and tone of voice can be indicators that things are going well – or very badly.

Communicating in a non-confrontational way helps prevent animosity in the first place, but consciously putting ourselves into the shoes of the 'enemy' does not come easily. Respect for the other person and for their feelings and needs can start reconciliation, or at the very least, open a negotiation that allows each to voice their feelings. But how easy is it to develop respect and to overcome the sense of the other party as the enemy? People or groups may need to move from: 'They killed our sons' to 'We mourn because we have lost our sons; they mourn because they have lost their sons; there should be no more deaths.' It was former Israeli Prime Minister Golda Meir who told Egypt's then President Sadat: 'We can forgive you killing our sons. We can never forgive you making us kill yours.'

People need enemies

In the 1980s, Vamik Volkan, psychiatrist, founder of the Center for the Study of Mind and Human Interaction (CSMHI) and citizen diplomat, was one of the first to suggest that we need 'enemies' to help us have a sense of our own identity, and to help maintain emotional equilibrium. He also highlighted the concept of 'otherness', the need to see and define 'The Other' as being different from us, allowing us to split our world into groups; the group to which we belong, 'us', and the other groups, 'them'.[4] The more difficult the circumstances that an individual or a society is facing, the more they will feel the need to have an enemy to blame and the more likely they are to follow a charismatic leader who demonizes the other group: the capitalists/the terrorists. The CSMHI draws on these theories in the hope of providing 'a vaccination for potentially antagonistic groups to reduce the likelihood that ethnic tensions will lead to violent conflict'. To date its work in Estonia (helping resolve ethnic splits between Estonians and the one-third of the population that is Russian and regarded as 'cuckoos in the nest') has been more successful than its original focus on Arab/Israeli relationships.

One problem with applying psychological insights to international conflicts is that the studies are mainly Western in their focus. The majority of all social science research around the world is based on samples of US undergraduates. To take just one issue: studies have shown that overcrowding leads to conflict in the US but is well handled in Dutch culture. But there are very few studies of such issues in Bangladesh or Indonesia.[5]

Defending ourselves

When relationships become antagonistic, psychological defenses come into play. In a quarrel we often see two defenses in action: denial and projection. We use denial – 'this is not happening' – to make life less unpleasant. There is often a wish for 'The Other' to be the same as us, to share our values and ideals. This is seen very often in couple relationships. If our partner does not or will not see the world the way we see it, this becomes intolerable and so we move to projection as a second defense.

Both individuals and civil or national groups use projection: one 'projects' one's own undesirable thoughts, motivations, desires and feelings onto someone else (usually another person, but can also be onto animals and inanimate objects) – such as when a child kicks the 'naughty' table which she bumped against: the bad feeling is projected onto the other, even the inanimate table, allowing us to feel 'it is their fault, not mine'.

Psychoanalysts suggest that we have always tended to blame our neighbors or a neighboring group for our own shortcomings.[6] When projection is coupled with denial, all sides in a conflict adopt an intransigent attitude; then the only possible outcomes are 'lose-lose', where no one is satisfied with the outcome, or 'win-lose'. Providing a space where people can take responsibility for their part in the dispute is essential, allowing them the opportunity to 'take back projections', to enter into a meaningful dialogue.

One way of looking at the links between individual psychology and violence is to see conflict as the result

---

Programmed for violence?

The Seville Statement on Violence notes that it is scientifically incorrect to say:

1 That we have inherited from our animal ancestors a tendency to make war. Although fighting occurs across the range of animal species, only a few cases of destructive intra-species fighting between organized groups have ever been reported among naturally living species.
2 That war or any violent behavior is genetically programmed into human nature... except for rare pathologies, the genes do not produce individuals necessarily predisposed to violence.
3 That in the course of human evolution there has been a selection for aggressive behavior more than for other kinds of behavior.
4 That humans have a 'violent brain'. How we act is shaped by how we have been conditioned and socialized. There is nothing in our neurophysiology that compels us to react violently.
5 That war is caused by 'instinct' or any single motivation.

And remember – the same species which invented war is capable of inventing peace. The responsibility lies with each of us. ■

of individuals' basic needs not being met.

An element of popular psychological belief, which is most unhelpful in conflict resolution, is the notion that humans are naturally aggressive and that therefore warfare is natural and even genetically predetermined. *The Seville Statement on Violence* (see box), which has been endorsed by UNESCO, sets out the best available information on the genetics of violence.

The Seville Group stressed that if humans, like some breeds of dogs and fighting birds, had really been bred for violence, we would be much more violent than we are. Commonly cited analogies between people and primates fail to acknowledge that the 'dominance' of the leader requires social bonding and affiliation skills as well as forcefulness and physical strength. Many earlier ideas about aggression in animals and humans were based on an individual model. Today there is much more awareness that humans and most mammals are inherently social creatures and that their behavior stems from what benefits them as members of social groups.

Chimpanzees for example practice reconciliation – friendly reunion between former opponents immediately after conflict. Elderly female chimpanzees also act as mediators. Such behaviors work to maintain valuable strategic relationships and parallels have been drawn between this primate behavior and the founding of the European Community to establish economic ties between countries which had been fighting for generations.[7]

Why has so much attention been devoted to animal aggression? Are peaceful animals simply too boring – who wants to study co-operation amongst cows?

If violence were indeed an inherent human attribute, then we would have to know why some humans are not at all violent, why some societies are much less violent than others and why whole regions of the

Mediation rules

Below are some of the key points in successful mediation.

The two core rules:
One person speaks at a time.
● No name-calling.

The basic process:
● Each party may make a short opening statement if they wish.
● Brainstorm a list of issues which must be decided before an agreement can be reached.
● Jointly decide on the order in which the issues will be discussed.
● Agreements on each issue are written down as they are achieved.
● Move onto the next issue until there are no more issues left.
● If more information is needed before a decision can be made, draft a 'to do' list.
● The mediator drafts a follow-up letter outlining agreements and what needs to be done before the next session.
● The next mediation session is scheduled.

The mediation style:
● Transformative and facilitative.
● Solution-oriented and reality-based.
● Direct and probing.

world seem to pass through periods of widespread conflict followed by relative peace.

The guidelines in the box *Mediation rules* hold good for international mediation, despite originating from professional divorce mediators. It can be seen why complex international peace talks take so much time, since just two people breaking up generally need several long sessions to work out the settlement.

Successful outcomes

Between 1945 and 1995 there were 131 international ethnic conflicts (the threshold for a conflict being at least 10 deaths). These resulted in at least 1,741 mediation events plus 614 negotiations, 9 arbitrations and 83 referrals to an international organization or multilateral conference. Out of these, 42 per cent of mediations were successful, at least for a while (defining success by the strict test of the achievement of a ceasefire or a partial or full settlement of the conflict).[8] The success rate does not appear to be affected by who was doing the mediation, whether an individual, an international organization, NGO or another state. Nor did the duration of a conflict have a major impact. However, mediations which took place before the violence began or in secret are hard to unearth and were excluded from this study. And although one might think that the earlier the mediation the better, this is not necessarily the case. Mediation tends to favor the status quo and thus if an aggressor has seized territory it may well reward him as originally happened in the break-up of Yugoslavia.

Some people argue that the UN is less successful in mediating conflicts now than it was in the early 1990s. In part this is because the easier conflicts have been solved and those which are left are intractable.[9] It is also increasingly true that unless the US backs such mediation, little can be done.

Some UN mediation success stories

- The conclusion of the Iran-Iraq War in 1998.
- Peace in El Salvador in 1994.
- The Paris Peace Accords of 1991 for Cambodia.
- Mozambique 1994, when RENAMO leader Alfonso Dhlakama threatened to pull the plug on the peace process by withdrawing from the elections but was persuaded to continue by the UN Special Representative, Aldo Ajello, who provided written UN guarantees that all complaints of election irregularities would be investigated.
- Guatemala Civil War Settlement 1996. The UN mediator, Jean Arnault, played a critical role in establishing sufficient levels of trust so that the parties could negotiate face to face.
- Tajikistan 1996 peace agreement/1997 power-sharing arrangement. ■

Source: F Hampson 'Can the UN still mediate?' in The *United Nations* and *Global Security* (2003).

Men and violence

In personal relations it is common to look at gender; however in international issues gender is usually neglected. Yet it is usually men who are the ones wielding the weapons or violating women and children. In Cyprus a cross-border NGO of Turkish and Greek Cypriot women got together to discuss the 'new state of affairs' possible under the UN Secretary-General's Plan for Cyprus. They began by envisaging the new relations between the two ethnic groups: equal, respectful, communicative and nonviolent but rapidly came to the realization that attaining such relations between men and women would bring considerably greater improvement in their lives.

HAD's very practical agenda includes getting women included in the peace negotiations; an end to military conscription; diversion of the defense budget to health, education and social services and the creation of a civilian-controlled police force with equal numbers of women and men. HAD supports a feminist perception of security: psychological, economic and social wellbeing free from the threat of war and the risk of harassment or violence at home, at work and on the streets. In many conflicts, as in Cyprus, women find that they can work across ethnic boundaries more easily than men because they have less personal investment in their ethnic identity: the 'chosen trauma and chosen glories' through which men recreate the past to justify fighting other ethnic groups.

Women who have been uprooted from their homes at marriage have already had to learn to live with one new identity and locality, which gives them greater flexibility. As the head of the Rwandan Unity and Reconciliation Commission Aloisea Inyumbana discovered, Rwandan women who had been raped and/or widowed found that these experiences gave them much in common; creating a unity more powerful

---

Cyprus: proving manhood

Since independence from Britain in 1960, Greek and Turkish Cypriots have been unable to agree over the political status of Cyprus and its links with Greece and Turkey. UN Peacekeepers have been there since 1963 but there was a Greek coup in 1974 which was followed by a Turkish invasion in the north of the island. There have also been further fatal incidents between the two sides.

In Cyprus as in many other countries, there is a norm that men 'prove their manhood' by violence. The people of Cyprus, and particularly women, have lived with the effects of violence and insecurity for decades. These have taken a heavy toll, not only in public life but also between individuals, including the relations of home and family. In HAD we detect a connection between gender-based violence at the personal level and the violence of armed conflict. There are clear links between the ideologies of militarism, patriarchy, nationalism and capitalism. Nationalist politicians and militaries need men 'to prove their manhood' by being willing to kill and die on behalf of the State. They need women to behave in ways required by patriarchal ideals; ready to offer up their sons and husbands in defense of the 'national interest'. ∎

Source: Hands Across the Divide (HAD).

---

than the divisions of ethnic identity which had been so brutally exploited for male-dominated political ends. They were also united in wanting outsiders to treat them with respect as individual people and not objectify them as 'victims of rape'.

Recruiting for peace

Conscription is a good example of the overlap between personal experience and social consciousness. In countries where men are conscripted they are deliberately trained into a militaristic culture which gives them new loyalties outside their families. Israel is unusual in conscripting women, but the genders are given separate roles. The abolition of conscription has diverse advantages: economic, social and psychological. An alternative could be to have conscription of young people into socially useful work such as building clinics and schools and helping to teach people to read. In the 1970s Nigeria had such a scheme for university graduates. The idea was that they would repay their student scholarships in this way and also that a planned ethnic dispersal, whereby each student worked with an ethnic group other than their own, would help to build national unity. Like many other dreams in Nigeria, the ideal was killed by the realities of corruption as richer graduates paid to avoid the scheme.

Whatever and wherever the discord, three points are vital for helping the parties to speak to one another: 1 The need for sufficient time to process issues; 2 An awareness of the history each party brings with them to the conflict; 3 A history of the particular situation.

Ambassador Hal Saunders is a former staffer of the US National Security Council, who runs workshops around the world on 'Sustained Dialogue'.[10] Currently he works with warring parties in Tajikistan and mentoring a black-white dialogue in Baton Rouge in the US.

After Israel's 1982 war on Palestinians in Lebanon Hal learnt the importance of 'political process' which could deal with people in pain. 'Everyone was living', said Hal 'on the frontiers of human suffering.'[11] Internationally he emphasizes that sustained dialogue works on a dual agenda: a) focusing on practical problems and issues of concern to all participants; and b) simultaneously and explicitly focusing on relationships that create and block the resolution of these problems.[12]

Psychologists' model

Believing that psychologists ought to be able to design a good model for resolving conflict, a group in Tasmania set to work. They created a scheme with four stages:

- developing expectations for win-win situations;
- defining each party's interests;
- brainstorming creative options;
- combining options into win-win situations.[13]

From divorce to war

While noting that there are many broadly similar models for resolving conflict which can all work, the psychologists stress that training in skills such as envisioning win-win solutions does markedly improve the ability to achieve positive outcomes (even seven years later). Once people start talking about their rights they tend to go down dead-end paths and lose their interest in solutions acceptable to both sides.

'We must wage peace'

There are two central views of what peace is: one is that the guns have stopped firing and the fighting has stopped; the other is that there can only be peace where there is also justice. The problem with this is that it leaves us without a word for the quiet after the battle. For women, children and men surrounded by guns, landmines and dead and maimed bodies this is a first and vital step. As the Dalai Lama said, 'Peace is not simply the absence of war. It is not a passive state of being. We must wage peace, as vigilantly as we wage war.'

The second step of attaining peace as true justice may well not have been reached anywhere in the world – it is an ideal to be reached for, not a daily experience. Wars where there is a clear winner are much less likely to break out again into fighting than wars where the two sides are fairly evenly balanced and the loser sees the prospect of reversing the decision by just one more battle.

The idea of the Just Peace is attractive but its practical implications can be very hard to agree on.[14] To take one issue, which is common to many refugee-return programs: what is the fair solution when refugees return to find that homeless people who have nowhere else to go have moved into their homes and farms? Is there a time limit beyond which expecting to take back one's house and land are unreasonable?

'The men stood over me and said "Let's shoot him" but the women joked with them and said "But he is so very thin and ugly – why waste a bullet?" So they let me live.'
  Andrew, a refugee who at the age of 8 and without his family walked from southern Sudan into Ethiopia and then into northern Kenya. He now lives in Australia. ■

Journey to peace

The UN's Educational, Scientific and Cultural Organization (UNESCO) deals with ideas and values rather than physical objects and so has been more controversial than some other UN bodies. Britain's Prime Minister Thatcher took the UK out of UNESCO because she considered it too left-wing. And while individuals may find its statements full of platitudes, many governments find its promotion of cultures of peace distasteful, probably because they are more comfortable with the culture of war.

UNESCO defined the elements of a war culture as: power characterized as the monopoly of force; having an enemy; hierarchical authority; secrecy and propaganda; armaments; exploitation of people and nature, and male dominance. However, this definition was not accepted by those member countries that saw themselves too clearly portrayed. The US delegate even complained that adopting a culture of peace would make it difficult to start a war.[15] The UN Culture of Peace involves eight main commitments: to respect all life; to participate in democracy; to preserve the planet; to reject violence; to rediscover solidarity; to share with others; to work for social equality, and to listen to understand.

It is the details that set fire to the debate. One UNESCO-sponsored multi-faith meeting declared that 'our ethical awareness requires setting limits to technology. We should direct our efforts towards eliminating consumerism'.[16] National projects to establish cultures of peace have been set up, starting with El Salvador, where the focus was on getting all sides

---

Peace at every level

Peace is:

Worldwide – The absence of war.

Regionally – A balance of forces in the international system.

Nationally – Positive: without structural violence.

Socially – Feminist: excludes violence also at the family and individual levels.

Economically – Holistic: includes the environment.

Personally – Spiritual: internal to each person. ■

---

working together on radio broadcasts to empower poor women, with the recognition that learning to work together was as important as the outcome. Funding was not easy. Like many other peace projects, workers in El Salvador found that even a tiny fraction of the funds previously devoted to fighting was hard to find – the one common factor between commercial radio stations and left-wing NGOs was the desire to be paid to promote peace.

Turmoil inside the nation-state

Violent conflict between individuals often falls into the domain of criminal law, and the victim can hope to have their day in court. However people caught up in civil unrest or international clashes usually do not have the opportunity to contribute to peace negotiations. The Balkan wars, Northern Ireland, Israel/Palestine, Cyprus and many of the African conflicts receive world-wide attention each time a new ceasefire is established or a new peace treaty signed. So why is the international community unable – or unwilling – to settle conflicts successfully? Our hesitation to intervene early in a brewing dispute to prevent violence is often the result of observing the four-centuries old ideal of state sovereignty. Many of today's conflicts are as old as colonialism and will not go away unless the state considers as its first obligation the protection of its citizens and their human rights.

Protecting human rights

Humanitarian intervention is often interpreted primarily as interference in internal matters of the state – since respect of national sovereignty relegates the international community to the role of spectator. It is not clear at what point public opinion changes and requests 'that something be done'; what is clear is that it takes considerable numbers of casualties to bring about this request.

This is not all: successful negotiations are hampered by several factors, not unlike those that prevent personal conflicts from being solved. Whilst mediation, the 'assistance of a neutral third party to a negotiation',[17] has been important in attempting to resolve conflicts internationally, external attempts by negotiators to mediate between warring internal factions are often futile because the outside mediator is thought to be unfamiliar with the details and complexities of the situation. Even worse, it is thought that an outsider cannot possibly share a compassion for the 'cause'. Negotiators (all men) like George Mitchell, Richard Holbrooke and Lord Owen have faced uphill battles to find suitable solutions and compromises for each side in a conflict – and not surprisingly failed in trying to implement a conflict management system across cultures.

Talking peace takes time

The time allowed for settling a conflict is crucial; often the deadlines are too tight. For example, the 2000 Camp David talks between Bill Clinton, Ehud Barak and Yasser Arafat were rushed in order to reach and finalize an agreement before the end of Clinton's presidency. Clinton was also accused of driving the negotiations to enhance his reputation as a 'peaceful' president.

In the Pacific region, the Bougainville negotiations were seen as much more successful than those for the

From divorce to war

Solomon Islands because no time limit was set for reaching agreement, and the New Zealand/Aotearoa hosts were in a relaxed 'however many participants, and as long as it takes' mode. Allowing time for dialogue is an important factor in healing psychological and emotional wounds.

Perceptions of the enemy take time to be adjusted; yet this point is often underplayed and ignored by the warring parties and the negotiators alike. Thus the resulting peace accords are at best temporary, such as the Oslo Accords of 1993 between the Israeli Government and representatives of the Palestinian Liberation Organization; the Dayton Accords (1995) over the Serb-Bosnian conflicts; the 1998 Northern Ireland Good Friday Agreement, and many others.

Peace agreements often only manage to freeze the status quo, so acting simply as a staging post between one conflict and the next. Peace is more likely to persist when there has been a clear winner in the fighting and the side which has lost, however aggrieved they may be, can clearly see that there is no point in renewing hostilities only to be trounced once more. Running conflicts as in the Basque region of Spain can persist for decades because nobody wins and nobody loses – except the blood-spattered corpses and their grieving relatives.

'Peace is really the playing and laughter of children, the babble of people saying freely what they think, and the scribble of pens, writing what the writers want to say. It is the music of people singing and dancing, people who have food, homes and love. It is people living without fear or lies.' *J Britton*, aged 10, in school essay, England. ■

1 L Kriesberg Constructive *Conflict from Escalation to Resolution* (Rowman & Littlefield 1998). **2** See I Parghi and B Murphy 'Gender and conflict resolution and negotiation: what the literature tells us' *Harvard University Working Papers, 1999.* **3** En.wikipedia.org/wiki/Ahimsa **4** V Volkan *The Need to Have Enemies and Allies, From Clinical Practice to International Relationships* (Aronson 1988) and *Blind Trust: Large Groups and Their Leaders in Times of Crisis and Terror.* **5** T Pettigrew 'Applying social psychology to international social issues' *Journal of Social Issues* Winter 1998 663-80. **6** A Bateman, D Brown and J Pedder *Introduction to Psychotherapy: an Outline of Psychodynamic Principles and Practice*, London: Routledge, Third edition, 2000. **7** F de Waal 'Evolutionary ethics, aggression and violence' *Journal of Law, Medicine & Ethics*, Spring 2004:18-24. **8** J Bercovitch 'Managing internationalized ethnic conflict: evaluating the role and relevance of mediation' *World Affairs* 166 Summer 2003, pp 56-72. **9** C Crocker ed. *Herding Cats: Multiparty Mediation in a Complex World* (USIP 1999). **10** H Saunders *A Public Peace Process: Sustained Dialogue to Transform Racial and Ethnic Conflicts* (St Martin's Press 1999). **11** H Saunders *Sustained Dialogue*, Presentation at Manukau City Council, November 2003. **12** ibid **13** J Davidson and C Wood 'A conflict resolution model' *Theory into Practice* 43, Winter 2004. **14** A quick web search will reveal a wide range of definitions: www.4justpeace.com/ is a Muslim site; www.ejjp.org/ is a Jewish site. **15** *Informals* 6 May 1999. **16** UNESCO 'The contribution by religions to the culture of peace' (Barcelona December 1994). See also E Boulding *Cultures of Peace: The Hidden Side of History* (Syracuse University Press 2000). **17** G Bingham *Resolving Environmental Disputes*, Washington DC: The Conservation Foundation, 1986, p 5, cited in J Bercovitch and J Rubin (eds) *Mediation in International Relations, Multiple Approaches to Conflict Management* (St Martin's Press 1992).

3 Culture clash

Of over one hundred armed conflicts in the years 1989-1996, only six were between states. The majority of today's civil wars are ethnic conflicts, where at least one party identifies itself by ethnicity.[1]

TODAY'S WARS ARE usually small but exceptionally brutal wars between fellow nationals divided along ethnic fault lines. Often ethnic concerns and economic disadvantages reinforce each other. This chapter discusses why this should be so and shows some of the techniques used to cross such cultural divides. This is a relatively new area and so there is still much to be learnt, especially about how to avoid imposing Western perspectives across the world.

Deep rifts along ethnic, racial, and cultural lines within nations are difficult to mediate. Since the end of the Cold War has removed many 'big brother' constraints on smaller countries, ethnic and/or intercultural conflicts have grown rapidly. For example, in 1996 alone, 14 of the 53 countries in Africa were engaged in fighting and 13 of these were internal rather than inter-state conflicts.[2] Internal warfare is often much more devastating than international because governments have little control over, and sometimes fuel, skirmishes that rage like bush-fires within their borders. Today, in international aggression a government which is losing, or indeed winning at too high a price, can usually find a way to stop fighting and back down with the support of neighbors and countries with economic interests in the region.

With internal conflicts, once the genie of violence is out of the bottle, it is very hard to put it back again. The government may be able to control its own supporters, but it usually has minimal influence over the opposition. Often, as civil conflict continues and both government and opposition forces split into

Deadly toll

In 2003 armed conflict remained a pervasive phenomenon. Africa and Asia hosted most wars – together accounting for more than 84 per cent of the total.

Source: Project Ploughshares 2004

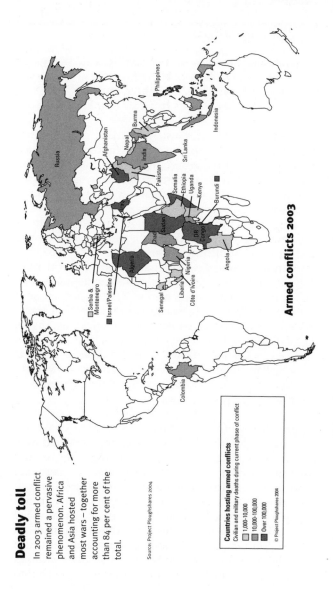

Armed conflicts 2003

Countries hosting armed conflicts
Civilian and military deaths during current phase of conflict

- ☐ 1,000–10,000
- ☐ 10,000–100,000
- ■ Over 100,000

© Project Ploughshares 2004

Culture clash

The Prophet's cloak

The Prophet Muhammad was approached by three groups quarrelling over which one would have the honor of setting in place the holy Black Stone at the Ka'aba in Mecca. The Prophet's response was to get his cloak and to ask each group to hold one corner whilst he put the stone on it so that they could all work together to lift it. ■

---

groups led by war-lords or gangs led by young militia men, it becomes ever more difficult to find leaders who can control those actually brandishing the guns, and who have taken to rape, pillage, looting and often to drugs – as seen in Sierra Leone and Afghanistan.

Although the terms are often used interchangeably, ethnic conflicts are those in which groups see themselves (or are seen by others) as sharing a distinctive and enduring collective identity based on a belief in a common origin, history and destiny. On the other hand, 'intercultural' conflict is a broader term also including religious strife which may divide citizens within a region such as Catholics and Protestants in Northern Ireland or Buddhists and Muslims in Thailand (where the Thai Muslims are a distinct and very dissatisfied minority).[3] Ethnic identity may be extended to include culturally specific practices and beliefs (such as female circumcision), physical appearance, language, and territory.

Against Islam?

The story about the Prophet's cloak (see box) was added to the training kit after a 12-year-old refugee trained as a peer mediator in Gaza asked: 'Is conflict resolution against Islam?' His grandfather had told him it was. A quick review showed that the course did not do enough to connect the concepts of tolerance, diversity and nonviolence with existing religious beliefs so that instead these ideas remained rootless and perceived as outsider, Western values. This incident is an object lesson in the need to make sure that universal values are grounded in local contexts. The idea of 'turning the other cheek' for example is often one which requires a great deal of explanation, not least in the Middle East.

Members of an ethnic group often join together for protection and to secure common interests but they may also be pressured into a new cohesiveness by discrimination from outside the group. As many autobiographies show, members of minorities often first come to take on minority group membership as a result of such outside pressure. It used to be a cliché of Australian life that Southern European identity was forged in school playgrounds as the *'dinkum* ['true'] Aussies' attacked those pupils who brought lunches more varied and interesting than the eternal white bread and Vegemite sandwiches. In a happy ending, students from a wide range of ethnic backgrounds now rejoice in mixed fillings for focaccias, naans and pita breads.

'They get all the good jobs'

Even where a conflict is labeled by outsiders and participants as 'ethnic' this may provide little indication of what the fighting is actually about. Civil conflict generally results from a deep level of emotional frustration. Members of group A are not antagonized by the mere existence of group B, they are annoyed and may turn to violence because they believe that group B is getting some form of unfair preferential treatment: 'they are taking our lands'; 'they get all the good jobs' and 'they are favored by the government'. Almost invariably the conflict is about scarce resources and who should get access to them, not about 'age-old' ethnic divides. Ethnicity is just a convenient way of defining 'them' and 'us' before determining the allocation of resources to the in-group and the exclusion or even forcible expulsion of the out-group. In some countries, India especially, caste replaces ethnicity for this purpose. In these cases the 'lower' groups are allowed to stay but at the cost of accepting that they will only be allowed to gather the crumbs that fall from the 'upper' groups' tables. In much of the Western world excluding people on the grounds of their ethnicity is no longer acceptable – but labeling people as potential terrorists fulfils some of the same functions.

Class warfare no more

As noted, tensions are created by unsatisfied structural needs such as access to resources, economic benefits, or political power. Intercultural conflict may arise as a result of:

- Discrimination or oppression of an ethnic group.
- Dissatisfaction of an ethnic group with its status in society.
- Poor economic conditions in society.

The decline of class-based politics is cited as one reason why tensions between different ethnic groups have risen in recent decades. The Communist system in Yugoslavia, for example, had done much to destroy class distinctions, leaving ethnicity as the best political lever for division. In Fiji, the class-based Labour Party succeeded in winning power through building a support base of both poor Indians and unemployed indigenous Fijians. This led to the 1989 coup by the deposed Fijian élite who pushed the line that all Fijians had the same anti-Indian interests irrespective of class.

Around the world, élites – by definition small groups – have an interest in promoting ethnic rather than class politics. In ethnic politics, members of the particular group are led to believe that the economy is failing, not because the leadership is as corrupt as it is incompetent, but because another ethnic group is grabbing an unfair share. This diverts attention away from the deficiencies of the élite and even makes poor members of ethnic groups happy to see the privi-leged grabbing the spoils of office: provided that the despoilers come from their own ethnic group. In the Fijian case, after the coup much international effort was devoted to trying to create an electoral system where parties would be obliged to garner support from both ethnic groups, but the model proved too complicated to work.[4]

'Taffy was a Welshman...'

In any conflict, people experience vulnerability and frustration. Where a dominant ethnic group gains political office, for example, it is a common percep-tion and experience that those public institutions, which are supposed to benefit everyone, are used to channel economic and political benefits largely to that group. Discrimination against under-dog group members, frequently portrayed as less deserving, often accompanies this preferential treatment. Such conduct often results from stereotyping. Members of the minority group are excluded from government employment because the majority view is that they are 'lazy and dishonest'. Such stereotypes are even spread by official text-books. For example, generations of British children learnt a rhyme which taught: 'Taffy was a Welshman, Taffy was a thief'.

Mohammed Abu-Nimer, director of the Conflict Resolution Skills Institute in Washington, describes working with groups of Arab and Israeli children who examined each other for the tails that they had been told they would find.[5] It is remarkable how often the ethnic prejudices of colonial powers who played favorites amongst their subjects, are still reflected in governmental hiring practices. The Baganda flourished in colonial Uganda because the British trusted them and the advantages they maintained after independence led to many of the ethnic tensions still found today.

Culture clash

Preferential access to education was the key.

Groups favored by the colonial powers were better educated and therefore, even with merit-based selection, could continue to grab the good jobs at independence.[6] This situation was made worse, as in Northern Nigeria and Ghana, where Muslim groups avoided Christian, missionary schooling and gained no alternative access to Western education. The Nigerian Civil War (1967-1970) was a direct consequence of the British colonial failure to spread educational opportunities equitably across the country's ethnic and religious groups. When the Soviets took control of the Ferghana Valley in Central Asia, they deliberately created boundaries that dispersed members of the same ethnic group such as the Tajiks, into different multi-ethnic regions. Afterward, the Soviet authorities were continuously being called upon to mediate disputes resulting from these artificial divisions. In this way, as noted in the book *War and Ethnicity*, 'ethnicity is socially constructed, it does not erupt suddenly and spontaneously but only in specific historical circumstances and... it is unlikely to become a lethal force except through the deliberate calculation of political elites.'[7]

Discrimination and oppression between and among different cultural groups often results in a loss of face when a particular group is so badly treated that it loses its positive identity.[8] Subordinate groups may endure discrimination for a while, until a sense of shared deprivation provides a basis for a political and/or social mobilization along ethnic lines. In South Africa, white Afrikaners, who were descended from Dutch and French settlers, viewed themselves as victims of British colonialism, even while using apartheid laws to oppress black South Africans. The Great Trek (1840s) and the later South African (Boer) wars were potent historical symbols which fuelled this sense of victimization. Afrikaners saw themselves as God's chosen people, redeemed by suffering, and destined to rule over the 'inferior' black Africans, Indians and Coloureds.

Sri Lanka's Singhalese majority also viewed themselves as victims. They resented the favorable treatment given to the educated and Christian Tamil minority in Jaffna and Colombo under colonial rule and conservative post-independence governments.

Social groups' perceptions of themselves play a crucial role in maintaining social order. Groups' histories become an important aspect of their folklore. Histories and norms become what defines a group and provides its identity.[9] Where a dominant culture relegates a second culture to an inferior role, simmering tensions can easily explode into violence. Being made to feel inferior and embarrassed to belong to a particular group every day of one's life will trigger strong animosity: 'We hate them for making us feel inferior – now we want to get our own back.'

Find a scapegoat

When national leaders fail to establish good governance, forge national integration and promote economic progress, this leads to poverty and unemployment, often resulting in communal, ethnic, religious and class conflict. The breakdown of social controls increases communal conflicts. A faltering or collapsed economy also contributes to tension and destabilization. And if the economic system offers unequal opportunities and unequal access to resources this will inevitably aggravate ethnic problems. Leaders

---

Eye for an eye

God offers Ivan a wish. However, there is a catch: 'Your neighbor will get twice what you get.' Ivan doesn't like the idea of his neighbor doing so much better so he finally asks God to blind him in one eye.

Variants of this grim parable are found in peasant societies from the Balkans to Mexico. ■

seek someone else to blame and minority groups, especially of successful traders such as the Chinese in South East Asia or the Indians in East Africa, are particularly vulnerable targets.

As Robert Muscat, author of *Investing in Peace*, says, 'Contrary to the assertions that conflict arises from political/ethnic/cultural causes, the real source of violent conflict can be traced to the *absence* of economic development that can eliminate extreme poverty and food insecurity'.[10] In the Australian schoolyard case cited before, tensions between earlier and later waves of immigrants were dampened by a flourishing economy in which there were jobs for all, and by annual immigration quotas which were deliberately linked to the availability of employment. Ethnic tensions in Australia have been most marked when and where there have been economic downturns and jobs have been in short supply.

Oil on the flames

Many countries have political and resource-led interests in DR Congo. Angola, Namibia, Zimbabwe and Sudan all backed Laurent Kabila's government, while Rwanda and Uganda fought his troops for control of the eastern region of Kivu.

The free-for-all over DRC's vast natural resources fuels the conflict. Some belligerents are using the state military budget to finance their involvement in the war while individuals close to the leadership plunder... All parties to the conflict are exporting minerals to defray war expenses... reducing the potency of donor leverage for peace.

Competition for land, resources and a favored position in a poverty-stricken environment fuels rivalries between Tutsi and non-Tutsi populations. The prevalence of minerals and export crops throughout rebel-controlled territories and the value of land in areas such as Masisi in North Kivu Province increases the stakes. Economic collapse and demographic pressure feeds insecurities and resentment, providing a fertile ground for recruitment into various military forces. ■

Source: J Prendergast and D Smock, *Putting Humpty Dumpty Together: Reconstructing Peace in the Congo* (USIP 1999).

It is difficult to think of cases of violent inter-ethnic conflicts in countries where there are flourishing economies which can deliver jobs and rising standards of living to the mass of the population. But a different trigger can result where there is a secessionist group which wants to form its own state. This often happens where the secessionists are indigenous to an area of rich natural resources and see themselves being much richer as citizens of an independent state which does not have to share its wealth with a range of much poorer provinces. The Indonesian province of Aceh for example has experienced bitter insurrection since 1976 because the Indonesian Government exploits the province's oil and gas but does not use this wealth to develop Aceh itself.

The way we do it here

Cultures have their own ways of dealing with conflict. In some cultures, confrontation or violence is commonly employed to resolve disputes. In others, differences may be tackled by using third parties or mediators. Where chieftaincy is the norm, discord may be settled by traditional leaders, although increasingly widespread education means that their authority is often challenged by the younger generation.

In yet other settings, rather than facing the issues, the parties simply retreat and let things take their course. This can complicate the situation and delay resolution where the various parties have different methods of handling disputes.

The British as colonialists found it much easier to deal with groups which had clear hierarchies and designated leaders (reflecting what they themselves were familiar with). They were quite thrown by groups such as the Igbo of Eastern Nigeria or the Solomon Islanders of the Pacific who had no single chief. So were British anthropologists who called them 'acephalous' or headless. In some cases the

Culture clash

British demand: 'Take me to your leader', resulted in the locals choosing someone on the spot just to keep the officials quiet – the colonialists were then puzzled when their system of indirect rule through getting the chiefs to pass on their orders was simply greeted by yawning non-compliance to the directions of the invented leaders.

All models for settling disputes within cultures require an understanding of the key differences before any attempts to ease tensions are begun. Europeans can well understand that Danes for example are very different from Spaniards or Italians; they also need to understand that on other continents the differences in cultures within a single country can be much greater than those between Scandinavians and Latins. Papua New Guinea for instance has a population of some five million people and over 800 languages (not just dialects but distinct languages with their own grammars and vocabularies).[11] Vanuatu in the Pacific has less than quarter of a million people but more than 110 languages scattered across chains of islands with different ecologies, cultures and systems of governance and inheritance. Unless the mediator knows the complexities involved, some interventions can set off a chain of unintended and unhelpful consequences. As the British colonial example has suggested, even establishing which community leaders people will actually follow (and therefore with whom to negotiate) is often a highly intricate task.

Understanding these differences is complicated by the fact that few ethnic groups still have a single

'Using trees as a symbol of peace is in keeping with a widespread African tradition. For example, the elders of the Kikuyu carried a staff from the thigi tree that, when placed between two disputing sides, caused them to stop fighting and seek reconciliation. Many communities in Africa have these traditions.' *Wangari Maathai* (1940-), founder of tree-planting Greenbelt Movement, Kenya, Nobel Peace Prize winner 2004, acceptance lecture. ■

culture (if they ever did, often male and female roles within it were remarkably distinct). In many societies now there is a tension between the leadership of the traditional chiefs or elders and the leadership of those who are younger and have had Western-style education, encouraging them to challenge the old order. Whilst there is much to be said for working with traditional leaders, it is also important to consider how far the views of women and young men have actually been taken into account in reaching a decision. Much of the terrible violence in Sierra Leone, where civil war erupted in 1991, is a result of younger men refusing to accept that life's rewards, including wives, should be the exclusive prerogative of the older generation (not that this excuses their behavior).

One positive aspect of violence – often raised by women speaking to startled Western observers who are not used to sentences that begin 'The good thing about the troubles is...' – is that for once they get to have their views taken into account. Across Africa women had been welcome participants in the struggles for independence and liberation but once an indigenous government came to power and the spoils of office were shared out, they were told in no uncertain terms to get back to their *shambas* (homesteads).

In the Pacific, women often banding together as groups of mothers have been effective peacemakers until their men move back to enforcing the traditional rules that women do not speak in public meetings. A peace negotiation may not seem to be the right place for outside negotiators to insist on gender equity, but it is still both unfair and unwise to ignore the principle that those who are most affected should have the greatest say. This applies not only to obvious gender issues such as the treatment of women who have been raped by the opposing side but also to such apparently gender neutral issues as the establishment of regional boundaries. In cultures where women marry men

Culture clash

from other villages and go to live with their husbands after marriage, boundaries can have far more impact on women than on men.

When people or communities are at loggerheads as a result of different needs and wants; varied beliefs; competing goals; divergent loyalties, values, ideologies, and geo-political factors, then the reconciliation process has to take them all into consideration.

Leave the guns outside, please

The skills needed to manage discord that can occur in communities and organizations focus on three main areas: in-depth knowledge; heightened mindfulness and awareness, and constructive skills for dealing with conflict.

While the acquisition of these skills does not mean that they are always going to be effective whenever they are used, people who have acquired them can make a considerable impact.

In any tense situation, there are different expectations from participants and from mediators. One mediator in the Somali peace talks in 1999 explained that it had taken six months just to get a common agreement that the parties would leave their machine-

Solomon Islands: two cultures in conflict

Harold Keke is a traditional leader who has attained mythical status in the civil violence in the Solomon Islands. He is alleged to have killed or ordered the killing of dozens of villagers and seven Anglican priests. Even after the arrival of a regional armed force to restore law and order, peace was unthinkable without the arrest and trial of Harold Keke. Understandably, however, Harold Keke felt no inclination to lay down his arms and surrender. He believed, almost certainly justifiably, that any Solomon Islander who arrested him would shoot him dead. Eventually he surrendered, but only after having been helicoptered out to an Australian ship where he knew that the Australians would have to ensure that, once arrested, he would be kept alive to stand trial. Still no-one knows what will happen once he is tried and presumably found guilty.

Since some Solomon Islanders continued head-hunting until the 1920s, it can be difficult to judge whether the traditional leader Harold Keke – who terrorized villagers by burying their leaders on the beaches up to their necks in sand – is a sane man reverting to the custom of his ancestors; a mentally unbalanced individual or just a politician who will stop at nothing to gain power. ∎

guns outside the negotiating room. Facilitators need to seek ways of getting both parties to validate the concerns of other groups and also be patient, humble, and willing to learn. No-one should assume that what individuals say is clearly understood by the other participants. Where possible, work in these settings should attempt to apply win-win negotiating principles rather than adversarial bargaining techniques.

Splitting the orange

The story of the sisters and the orange (see box) is used to illustrate the point that there is a difference between interests (what you really want) and positions (what you say you want). Many negotiations break down because people adopt incompatible positions – whilst if they were prepared to discuss their interests they could reach an agreement which would satisfy both sides. A common example is where a minority group says that it wants complete independence from its parent country. But the reason for wanting independence is the desire for increased political control and improved social and economic status – goals that could be achieved through autonomy rather than complete independence.[12] A specific example of this approach applies to the Sikhs and Hindus in the Punjab. Sikhs say they want independence and more access to water whilst Hindus say they want a united India and equal sharing of water resources; but both can agree on wanting prosperity for the Punjab and less terrorist activities and fighting.[13]

Speaking in tongues

Language differences are often a major factor in ethnic flare-ups. Yet scant attention is paid to this, partly because participants from outside rarely speak a local language. Although Somalis share a common language, they are so aware of the importance of how words are used that the clans include poets on their official negotiation delegations both as respected figures and because of their potential to propose helpful phrasing. Lawyers play a similar role on many Western delegations, meeting the second criterion if not the first. Anyone who doubts the importance of getting the wording right can imagine the difference between having to tell a government minister, sitting behind his mahogany desk with his armed bodyguards outside, that he should 'stop being corrupt' or that 'the government should be open and transparent'. Corruption has been much more coherently addressed in bilateral diplomatic talks since the alternative expression 'transparency' has come into

---

Two sisters and an orange

Two sisters are fighting over the only orange in the house. Their mother arrives to arbitrate. Instead of giving them half each, she asks why they want the orange. One wants to drink the juice whilst the other wants the skin to make a scent. So the mother can give both sisters exactly what they want. ∎

Palestinian-Israeli dialogue

A mediator working with Israeli Jews and Palestinian Muslims asked for reactions to drawings of a swastika and a star of David.

	Israelis	**Palestinians**
Swastika	Still terrifying	Sad but 'old history'
Star of David	Warm identity symbol	Symbol on the tank that flattened my father's house last week

Then they moved to a thought exercise, not 'Palestinians are terrorists' but 'Why do Palestinians commit terrorist acts?'

Source: Pittsburgh Middle East Peace Forum

fashion.[14] Former US Ambassador McDonald told the story of trying to bring 'conflict resolution' to Russia only to find that the term was virtually untranslatable in a culture that was habituated to government by force and power. Russians now talk about 'conflictology'.[15]

Decoding the message

Differences of language are not just a matter of words. Messages have both form and content and the recipient has to correctly decode the message. However the greater the cultural distance between 'encoder' (speaker) and 'decoder' (recipient), the greater the difference between the message as sent and the message as received.[16] People sharing a culture have more or less the same frame of reference; those from somewhere else will have different reference points, especially if they have been on different sides in a civil war.

One of the key contrasts is between individualistic cultures and those which emphasize interdependence and collective identity. In collectivist ones, communication is very sensitive to the context. There is a strong emphasis on politeness, relationship-building, tact and indirectness. Individualistic cultures on the other

hand de-emphasize the context and personal relationships and concentrate on the message. Communication is direct and explicit, with little rhetoric, allu-
sion or complex etiquette. There are also very different
attitudes to time. For Westerners there are often regi-
mented schedules, haste as a virtue and an emphasis
on the future. For some non-Westerners the tendency
is rather for gradual flow of time in cycles and seasons
independent of human wishes; patience is a virtue and
the past lives on in the present.

The supposedly universal models of negotiation
used by diplomats mostly reflect an individualistic,
Western, impatient approach. The instrumental style
which separates people from issues and prioritizes
creating efficient, maximally beneficial outcomes will
often seem very foreign to cultures which prioritize
human relationships and distrust urgency.

What is negotiable and what is not is also very much
culturally determined. However all countries value
national pride and have symbols of great power. That
said, feelings about particular symbols vary and, for
example, other English-speakers who cheerfully wear
their flag on their underpants are puzzled by some
Americans' desire to make burning the flag a criminal
offense. In negotiations, former colonies may have a
special sensitivity to the presence of foreign military as
observers or peacekeepers, especially if they come from
the former colonial power; alternatively such troops
may be seen at least to have the virtue of familiarity.[17]
Even the stages of a negotiation are culturally defined.
Groups with high value on personal relationships
often work to set up a rich network of associations
before serious negotiations begin. In one instance, the
Japanese appreciated an American negotiator who
devoted one visit to simply getting to know people – not
raising any substantive points at all. Groups who value
'face' try and avoid uncertainty, surprises and crises.
Other groups are more open to new elements.

Putting on the style

In general, the US/West's goal-oriented style of negotiating can differ widely from those found elsewhere on the globe.

Western style – individualistic, *eg us*	High culture – collectivist, *eg China*
Quickly down to business	Establish networks first
Relatively anonymous, informal	Personal, formal
Parties take turns in speaking	Most important speak first
Set out opening position	Ask for concessions from the other side
Start with facts, move to principles	Start with principles, apply to case at hand
Bargain/ haggle over details	Move slowly but on big issues not details
Power diffused	Power at the top
Aggressive, impatient	Polished, measured
Will say 'no'	Can say 'maybe' or 'yes, of course' and mean 'no'
Push for conclusions – take best material offer	Need face-saving alternatives above material gain
Focus on each stage – this year	Focus on the whole process – next 100 years.

The box on negotiating styles sets out differences between Western and High Culture negotiators based on the experience of Americans with the Japanese and Chinese (often Europeans might be in between the two extremes).[18] In negotiating with Arab parties, for example, Westerners would do well to consider using a non-aligned Arab mediator because most Arabic cultures value trust more than neutrality, and thus many Arabs would prefer even a partial insider over a neutral outsider. As to negotiating with rebel militias in the red dust of tropical Africa, we do not yet really know enough to compile a comparable table, although extreme patience is clearly required.

Where ethnic tensions arise as a result of poor economic conditions, the best negotiating skills may prove worthless. However, working together to create structural changes that tackle issues of exclusion and marginalization is always worthwhile. Where there is political will and everyone is given the chance to participate, then directing efforts towards some common goal, which neither conflicting group can achieve individually, often provides the best way forward. An example of this is where both sides want to re-open the only sea port to get trade moving, and work to this end with a donor who will fund the necessary building works. This engages both parties productively without requiring a personal moral transformation first.

In the Middle East it has been suggested that collaboration on water projects can help to bring peace. Israel is to sell water and electricity to Palestinians in the Gaza strip in return for offshore natural gas. British Gas, which owns the rights to natural gas reserves near Gaza, is seeking to sell natural gas in Israel to the value of $3.5 billion. The last time the Palestinians made a bid for an Israeli natural gas tender, the Israeli Government chose to buy from Egypt instead, but now the thawing of relations with the Palestinians may make Israel keen

---

Sulewesi: overcoming religious divides

In Sulewesi, Indonesia, the healing program began by bringing each community together to discuss their feelings about the conflict: their hatreds, insecurities and suspicions. Poso is a very religious area – primarily Christian or Muslim with small Buddhist and Hindu minorities, so staff worked closely with local religious leaders, garnering their support... Volunteers were selected to receive training in community healing which was done through discussion, sports, arts and an alternative school for children whose school had been destroyed. Visits were arranged between Christian and Muslim communities ...they reached a common understanding that they are all victims and all headed for the same aim: peace. During the August 2002 flare-up a particular Muslim village once known as hard line refused to get involved in attacking Christians, and initiated discussion with their neighbors to try and reduce the use of violence. ■

Source: *Oxfam Horizons* 2 (4) December 2002.

to bolster the economy of Gaza before their withdrawal. Meanwhile Israel and Jordan have agreed to build a joint canal between the Red Sea and the evaporating Dead Sea.

One review of experience in Kosovo, in the Balkans, suggests that there are six ways of closing the cycle of violence:

1 Pursue restorative justice, including punishing the guilty but also providing for rehabilitation and letting the innocent clear their names.
2 Use emotional healing.
3 Use forgiveness.
4 Draw a line under the past.
5 Use compensation and reparations to facilitate social and economic development.
6 Pursue truth through dialogue (not through a Truth and Reconciliation Commission at this stage, since until the future status of Kosovo is determined and people are genuinely seeking a basis for future co-existence, such a Commission could simply act as a forum for propaganda by both sides and thus could lead to more conflict).

Ethnic conflicts with good outcomes

Below are listed some conflicts which generally ended positively, although of course some people or groups may not be pleased with every aspect.

- 1971 Bangladesh becomes a state
- 1988 Matignon Accords recognize rights of indigenous population
     of Kanaky (New Caledonia)
- 1992 the end of apartheid in South Africa
- 1992 Mozambique Peace Settlement
- 1990s Germany redefines citizenship to include Turkish immigrants
- 1998 Good Friday Agreement in Northern Ireland
- 2002 Independence of East Timor/Timor Leste
- 2006 ? Peace in Afghanistan

Culture clash

Violence had flared in Kosovo in 1996 between Albanian-Kosovar separatists and the Serbian and Yugoslav security forces. In 1999, NATO bombed Yugoslav targets, while Albanian fighters continued fighting Serbian forces and Kosovan Serb civilians. Progress since then has been patchy. War criminals fled. Serbs who stayed in their turn became stereotyped victims of violence. An effective police force was not established quickly enough to prevent this hostility. The UN force (UNMIK), did not have enough set procedures to deal with urgent matters such as accusations of war crimes against its own locally engaged staff. Too many international NGOs were offering culturally inappropriate trauma counseling.

The assumption underlying such projects is that the experience of war and bereavement has produced a psychological disorder: trauma – to be treated by Western talk-therapies – rather than a rational response of anger and grief which requires the re-establishment of social networks and support-systems, or even jobs and homes to go to. Psychologists noted on the file of a man who had had his jaw shot away that he was 'inappropriately angry' but who were they to judge? Some good things are happening: former combatants who attacked Roma/gypsies have built a Roma Resource Centre; and Albanians and Serbs together have rebuilt a city park.

The international community has been blamed for being too slow and for doing the wrong things but many Kosovar-Albanians have also been unforgiving and little concerned for the human rights of all ethnic groups. There have been challenging suggestions for reframing identity away from ethnicity to focus on gender, generation and occupation instead. There is

'Never surround your enemy on all four sides – for someone will get hurt, most probably you.' *Mao Zedong* (1893-1976), Chinese leader, responsible for millions of deaths in China. ∎

also a movement to create a collective memory that admits wrongdoing on all sides, makes heroes of those who stood out against the violence of their own side and enshrines the worth and human rights of all.[19]

1 Based on M Sollenberg and P Wallansteen *States in Armed Conflict 1996* (Department of Peace and Conflict Research, Uppsala University 1997). **2** Y Tandon, *Root Causes of Peacelessness and Approaches to Peace in Africa*, at: http://www.seatini.org/reports/roots.htm **3** DH Akenson *Small Differences: Irish Catholics and Irish Protestants* (Gill and Macmillan 1991). **4** S Prasad and D Snell 'Enabling Civic Capacities for Conflict Prevention and Peace-building' *Searching for Peace in Asia-Pacific*, by A Heimanns, N Simmonds and H van de Veen (Lynne Riener & Boulder 2004). **5** 'Children, diversity, religion and conflict' Keynote Speech for GNRC Maryknoll, New York, 12 May 2002. **6** R Leith and H Solomon *On Ethnicity and Ethnic Management in Nigeria*, at: http://www.accord.org.za/ajcr/2001-1/accordr_v2_n1_a5.html. **7** D Turton ed *War and Ethnicity* (Transaction 1997) p 10. **8** S Ting-Toomey and J Oetzel. *Managing Intercultural Conflicts Effectively*, (Sage 2001). **9** See J Mertus *Kosovo: How Myths and Truths started a War* (University of California Press 1999). **10** R Muscat *Investing in Peace: How Development Aid can Prevent or Promote Conflict*, (ME Sharpe 2002). **11** For more information, see http://www.cia.gov/cia/publications/factbook/geos/pp.html. **12** See www.beyondintractability.org/m/interests.jsp **13** R Fisher, E Kopelman and A Schneider 'Look behind statements for underlying interests' in *Beyond Machiavelli: Tools for Coping with Conflict* (Harvard University Press 1994: 39-40). **14** See Transparency International www.transparency.org/ **15** J McDonald 'The need for multi-track diplomacy', *Centre for Development Research* (ZEF) (Bonn 2000), Paper 9. **16** L Szalay 'Intercultural communication – a process model', *International Journal of Intercultural Relations*, 1981(5). **17** R Cohen *Negotiating across cultures: communication obstacles in international diplomacy* (USIP 1991). **18** Cohen, see note 12. **19** From M Randle's review in *CCTS Newsletter* 16 of H Clark's *Kosovo Work in Progress: Closing the Cycle of Violence* (Coventry University 2002).

4 Working diplomatically

Diplomacy still plays a major role in preventing and resolving conflict, often in areas such as trade rules and breaches of human rights conventions.

'AN AMBASSADOR IS an honest man who is sent to lie abroad for the good of his country,' commented British diplomat Sir Henry Wooten in the 17th century, and some might say nothing much has changed. Traditional diplomacy consists of interactions between governments. Professional diplomats talk on behalf of their governments to their counterparts, with each striving to advance their own national interests; not necessarily concerned either to advance the common good or to promote peace. Diplomats speak from a 'brief' with instructions from their political masters, which defines the official position and tells them what their government can or cannot accept. As their biographies show, usually the more senior the diplomat, the more latitude she/he has to stretch the limits and even to suggest new compromises.

Whilst many diplomats are career bureaucrats some are also direct political appointees – often 'wild cards' with the ability to speak directly with the powers at home to get policies changed or to ensure the allocation of resources to back up new initiatives. Western governments that want their diplomats to lie prefer to keep them in the dark – as happened with Adlai Stevenson, former US Ambassador to the UN, who was excluded from US Cabinet discussions of the 1961 Bay of Pigs invasion of Cuba.

For autocratic rulers, such as Saddam Hussein, it makes sense to appoint close relatives or political allies as diplomats to ensure that they represent the ruler's interests, especially in personal financial matters, and do not defect whilst overseas or let considerations of genuine national interest influence their dealings with other governments.

Talk does save lives

Diplomacy often seems to be talking for talking's sake and sometimes it is. 'Diplomats don't have to understand something to tell you about it,' goes the saying. But so long as diplomats keep talking, there is a chance of heading off the fighting. It is sometimes possible to calculate the number of lives saved by 'just talking' as, for example, where a conflict has averaged so many deaths each year over a number of years and then talks begin and the number of deaths plummets. Calculations for Northern Ireland show that until the IRA cessation of violence in 1994 some 100 people were killed each year.[1] In the next seven years about 100 people were killed overall, representing a saving of 600 lives over the period.

Conversely, the collapse of the Middle East Peace process in 1999 resulted in at least 700 deaths, which may not have occurred if the talks had continued. In countries such as Sri Lanka where the annual death toll is much higher, the saving of lives through keeping negotiations alive could be in the order of tens of thousands each year.

Words do matter

To outsiders diplomats seem to spend vast amounts of time talking about insignificant differences in wording. Yet words do matter. 'Genocide' is an excellent case in point. Once an action is defined as genocide within the UN system then the 136 countries which are signatories to the Convention on the Prevention and Punishment of the Crime of Genocide are obliged to take action to prevent and punish it.[2] Under obligations that they have themselves taken on, they have no choice; they must act. Hence the extreme reluctance to use the actual word 'genocide' and the current debates about its use in reference to Darfur in Sudan.

Countries that do not want to see intervention to protect people who are being wantonly killed are motivated by a fear that intervening in Sudan, for example, could justify intervention in their own countries. The matter is further complicated by oil deals made with the Sudanese Government. For example, China is concerned both about possible intervention in its own backyard, Tibet, and about access to Sudan's oil.

Threatening behavior

War is callously said to be just diplomacy by other means. We can never know what might have been, and whether better diplomacy could actually have averted war. One of the commonest errors is for one side to give the other a warning that is not perceived as being credible. Any country, threatening another, has a duty to ensure that they only make threats which are believable and which are believed. At the time of the first Gulf War in 1991 for instance, Saddam Hussein apparently did not believe that the US would intervene. Whether the Ambassador concerned, April Glaspie, was at fault or whether she was just the chosen fall guy, this was a major error in diplomacy.

Similarly, the First World War could have been prevented if all the countries and leaders involved had had a realistic understanding of how the others would react to the onset of violence and who would feel obliged to support whom. There is an old joke that says that the only way the Second World War could have been prevented would have been if Germany had won the First World War. However diplomacy did stand a realistic chance of preventing Italy joining in on the German side.

Flags and red faces

At one stage of the Cambodian Peace talks in 1990 one of the parties was accidentally invited to sit behind the flag representing their sworn enemy. The consequence was an immediate walkout; some very red diplomatic faces, much leafing through books of flags and endless talking to get all parties back around the table. At least they had already agreed on the shape of the table: round tables are much more conducive to alliances and agreements than oblong tables which have a head and tail and pit opposing sides against each other.

Symbolism and role-playing are very important in diplomacy. Around the world there are Western diplomats with firm instructions that they cannot talk to or recognize representatives of the State of Palestine as such, but that where the Palestinian is the longest-serving diplomat and thus the Dean of the Diplomatic Corps, then they may talk to her or him, in their role as Dean and chief representative of all diplomats in the country. Andrew Young, when US Ambassador to the UN, was allegedly fired the day after breaking the formal diplomatic rules by having coffee with a member of the PLO Observer Delegation.

In many conflicts a key question is who actually represents the legitimate government of the country (think of Cambodia, China/Taiwan, Somalia). 'Terrorists' are only terrorists until they get into government. Most members of the current South African Government were once officially listed as terrorists by both Britain and the US. As independence was achieved across Africa, more and more former terrorists or freedom fighters came to power and went to visit the British Queen at Buckingham Palace.

Several Israeli ministers have also been former terrorists including Menachem Begin and Yitzhak Rabin. One distinctive feature of the current 'War on Terror' is that the terrorists may aspire to change

'Since wars begin in the minds of people, it is in the minds of people that the defenses of peace must be constructed.' UNESCO Constitution (1945). ■

Working diplomatically

> 'I have doubts about how far terrorism can be uprooted. We were also terrorists once and they didn't uproot us and we went on dealing in terrorist activities... If you wait and see until there is 100 per cent success in uprooting terrorism, it appears to me that peace will get farther and farther away before our very eyes.' *Lea Rabin*, Yitzhak Rabin's widow in a radio broadcast 10th September 1997. ■

governments and ultimately to rule the world, but to date they have not aspired to take over the specific governments of the countries where they attack.

Diplomats generally only talk to accredited representatives of recognized governments. This makes for difficulties where there are rebels who have taken power or provinces which have seceded. Apart from the break-up of the former Soviet Union and the former Yugoslavia, Bangladesh and Timor Leste/East Timor are rare recent cases of having achieved statehood by breaking away from a larger country.

Diplomats hardly ever earn much sympathy, but those members of the profession who have to keep a straight face whilst explaining that Timor Leste/East Timor deserved independence from Indonesia whilst West Papua, with an even stronger historical case, does not, ought to be given credit for casuistry under fire. Some governments recognize regimes, others recognize countries. As successful coups have become more frequent more governments have moved to simply recognizing countries. The implicit rule should be that the legitimacy of governments stems from the consent of the governed – but establishing this point can be extremely demanding and would leave numerous countries without legitimate governments.

No rules to this game
Traditional diplomacy relies upon countries being willing to abide by the rules. It is much more difficult in conflicts within sovereign states where there are no agreed boundaries to the negotiation game. Yet

sometimes internal talks could stop civil war, as perhaps in Chechnya.[3] Or international diplomacy might have been effective as in the case of Bougainville where Australia could have worked harder to persuade Papua New Guinea to allow much more autonomy to Bougainville at an earlier stage.

The extent to which factional leaders aspire to become leaders of existing or new breakaway states is an important factor. In the case of Angola, rebel UNITA leader Jonas Savimbi was never going to stop fighting before he became President and he had international backers in the West who supported him for ideological and economic reasons. In fact he was killed in 2002, still fighting government troops despite having been offered the vice-presidency.

The value of statehood

In the current international system of sovereign nation states there is unique value in leading a government. The head of an Indian state or a Chinese province may govern a 100 million people, far more than most sovereign states, but he/she arguably has far less power than the head of a national government for a million people. All national governments, however few their citizens, can have a seat at the UN; they also have the power to make deals based on the control of the state and the ability to commit the country as a whole.

In some cases, formal diplomacy plays a vital role in getting agreement to end international support for a war. It is rare for an insurgent group to be able to survive without support from outside, whether from the proceeds of selling off 'looted' resources; from the funds sent home by emigrants and/or support from regional neighbors.

Bad neighbors

Neighboring countries that become involved in internal disputes often do so to support a related ethnic group, as well as for direct economic benefits and/or in hopes of adding to their own national territory. There seems to be no rebel group, however abhorrent, that cannot find a neighboring country to provide support to promote its own strategic ends.

A good example of this is Sudan's support of the Lord's Resistance Army (LRA), the group that terrorizes parts of Northern Uganda through kidnapping children from their villages and forcing them to become child soldiers and sex slaves. However, in this case the Ugandan Government is also implicated in allowing the rebellion to continue. Both the Government and the army gain some advantages by having the rebels keep the North in turmoil, so that region is excluded from the contest for political power in the South where the capital and the bulk of the national wealth are located.

There is debate as to how far rebel groups are motivated by 'greed or grievance'.[4] Many such groups are aggrieved by exclusion from the political process, and in the poor countries where they mostly operate, greed may mean no more than gaining a modest control over the necessities of life. Where the insurgents are motivated by reasonable grievances, international diplomacy can also play a role by pressuring the national government to address their concerns.

Nip it in the bud

Ideally diplomacy should avert fighting and death. 'Preventive diplomacy' means just that: heading off severe disputes between states; preventing these from escalating, and if they do, limiting the intensity of violence and humanitarian problems as well as trying to stop them spreading geographically. Such diplomacy often works alongside measures to build confidence so that previously hostile or mutually suspicious parties and governments get used to working together.

But of course there are difficulties. For example, when

> 'A peacemaker often receives wounds.' Yoruba saying (Benin, Nigeria, Togo). ■

government officials are involved, preventive diplomacy runs the danger of deviating from the respect for national sovereignty and non-interference in a state's internal affairs. The 1999 report of the Council for Security Co-operation in the Asia Pacific Region bristles with such concerns but also notes Indonesia's work as a facilitator in the dispute between the Philippine Government and the rebel Moro National Liberation Front. Other examples included the ASEAN Troika experience in Cambodia, and the Thai/Malaysia Joint Development Area (which aims at preventing conflict by promoting joint development in a disputed territory).

All in all, there is reasonable evidence that preventive diplomacy used early enough does work and saves both lives and also the money which would have been needed for humanitarian aid and rebuilding infrastructure.[5]

Where groups of countries need to act in concert, often it is only diplomacy that can create the necessary glue. Attempts at setting up economic sanctions for example reveal how hard it is to deal with a wide range of national interests, especially where some countries are being asked to act against their own economic wellbeing. At a minimum, sanctions should cut off the supply of arms to warring countries and to factions within countries – yet all too often arms-trading countries will continue regardless. US diplomatic failures and fear of communism prolonged civil war in Angola for decades.[6] And the biggest diplomatic failure of today – the inability to achieve peace between Israel and Palestine – is set in a context where Israel and the US stand almost alone in most relevant votes in the UN General Assembly.[7]

Some of the most intricate and lengthy negotiations have been around disarmament. Getting countries and people to put down their weapons requires a high degree of trust all round. And in contrast to disarmament, how to stop people arming in the first place? To take a specific new example: how to prevent terrorists accessing the materials to mount a nuclear attack? Only concerted international diplomacy could find out who, where, when and how to stop them.

Balkans failure

The break-up of Yugoslavia is a clear example of the failure of preventive diplomacy.[8] Peacemaking did not succeed because the West wanted two incompatible things: unity and democratization. The West's threats of withholding economic aid failed because they were not credible or united and also because the warring factions were prepared to put physical security and group identity above economic prosperity. A more controversial reason given for this failure is that in ethnic conflicts cure may actually be easier than prevention.

One form of preventive diplomacy, which is often neglected, is providing dictators with a face-saving exit – this can often prevent violence breaking out or bring it to a close. As Head of State in Nigeria, General Yakubu Gowan, who had been victorious in the civil war, exercised such diplomacy on his own account telling restive young military officers: 'If you are going to stage a coup, at least do it when I am out of the country, that way no-one gets killed.'

Even where dictators are prepared to quit, they often face the difficulty that if they stay in their own country their victorious enemies may try and kill them and their families and will certainly try and seize their wealth, so they need to find somewhere else to 'retire' to – for example, Uganda's strongman Idi Amin fled in 1979 and looked after his chickens in Saudi Arabia until his death in 2003. Finding a home for unwanted dictators can be one of diplomacy's more valuable tasks in terms of preventing bloodshed. Subsequent international legal proceedings can then be used to try former dictators for their crimes in office and to pursue their illicitly gained wealth.[9]

And when preventive diplomacy is not enough, there is coercive diplomacy. Former US Secretary of State George Shultz argued that 'the hard reality is that diplomacy not backed by strength is ineffectual'. In the words of former Stanford University emeritus professor Alexander L George, 'the general idea of coercive diplomacy is to back one's demand on an adversary with a threat of punishment for non-compliance that he will consider credible and potent enough to persuade him to comply with the demand'.[10] Coercive diplomacy is a high-risk strategy: the US threat of an oil embargo if Japan did not withdraw from China resulted in Pearl Harbor. But it worked in the 1962 Cuban missile crisis where the Soviet Union did withdraw its ballistic missiles. This is also a strategy which only works with targets that can be relied upon to react in a way the West expects; it may well

Divided peoples

Most fighting today is between groups within a state, rather than between states. Such clashes are often over control of government or territory. Since 1989 there has been a trend towards separatist conflicts. Violence can flare over issues such as unstable government and disputes over natural resources (as in sub-Saharan Africa); over border issues and ideological/religious differences, to ethnic tensions (as in regions of the former USSR: Nagorno-Karabakh, Georgia, Northern Caucasus, Moldova and Tajikistan). The world's most warring region is still the Middle East, with almost half of its countries involved in fighting. Other hot spots are North Korea-South Korea, China-Taiwan, Central Africa, Kashmir and the Caspian region.

Percentage of countries in region with armed conflicts, 1997

- ■ Middle East
- Africa
- Asia
- ■ The Americas
- □ Europe

2%
5%
24%
26%
43%

not work with North Korea, for example, or another country that has different parameters.

In today's world there are still many situations where diplomacy can be effective, especially in the Middle East and Africa.

Routes of diplomacy

As already noted, most armed conflicts are no longer wars between nations but within national boundaries. By 1987 only four of the world's major clashes were cross-border, the rest being civil wars or internal wars of independence. Ten years later there were no full-blown international wars but 24 civil conflicts. The UN Charter specifically prohibits its intervention in disputes within sovereign states and there is no alternative intergovernmental organization to intervene. UN agencies and NGOs can provide economic and humanitarian aid but only with at least the tacit approval of the national government in power. Sadly, however, most forms of this aid do little to resolve the root causes of such conflicts and can actually do harm where they fail to be totally equitable.[11] 'Track One' (government-to-government) diplomatic efforts are not designed to resolve root causes of conflict but to deal with the existing balance of power.[12] And of course much 'diplomacy' has nothing to do with the diplomatic corps. See the box *Tracking diplomacy* for the differing approaches.

In contrast to the black tie/gin and tonic formality of Track One diplomacy, Track Two is informal, between citizen groups aimed at reducing discord by dampening down anger, fear and tensions and by improving communication and mutual understanding. Often Track Two work paves the way for Track One to take over the detailed brain and legwork of securing agreement on a binding treaty, once the public has been convinced of the need for control. Good examples include the Treaty to Ban the Use of Land

Tracking diplomacy

Below are the main levels and people involved in working to end conflicts.

Track 1: official government-to-government diplomatic interaction.
Track 2: unofficial, non-governmental, analytical efforts by skilled, experienced and informed private citizens directed towards solving difficulties and creating policies.
Track 3: business-to-business, private sector, free enterprise, multinational corporation interactions.
Track 4: citizen-to-citizen exchange programs of all kinds – scientific, cultural, academic, student.
Track 5: media-to-media work to educate people about the ideas/culture/needs of the group they are in conflict with.
Track 6: Education and training.
Track 7: Peace activism.
Track 8: Religion.
Track 9: Funding.
[Track 10: Use of the internet to promote peace.]

The work follows these phases:
1 Exploration of subject and self.
2 Analysis and involvement.
3 Follow through.
4 Disengagement and aftermath.

Source: Based on L Diamond and J McDonald *Multi-Track-Diplomacy: a Systems Approach to Peace*, 1991. ∎

Mines and developments towards a treaty restricting the spread of small arms (which have created armies of child soldiers).[13]

Another example would be the campaign to force multinational corporations exploiting natural resources to 'say what you pay', revealing funding to governments and rebel factions alike.[14]

Because the nature of war and therefore of peace has changed, so too must diplomacy. This applies both to the content covered as well as to the contacts made. Nowadays, diplomats spend much of their time on trade issues. At the formal legitimate end there are matters such as the World Trade Organization (WTO) negotiations but at the other extreme are dealings to cut off illicit trades in diamonds, minerals, timber and oil which rebels use to raise the money to buy arms. While the rebels can be seen as brutal and unprincipled, those buying the diamonds and other goods are also implicated in bloodshed.

'Naming and shaming' is used by some to highlight corporate activities in countries where sanctions are operating or human rights are abused, such as Cambodia, Angola (where De Beers for example has mined diamonds), Sierra Leone, Liberia, Afghanistan, the DRC and Somalia. This can result in the withdrawal of some states and international corporations to protect their reputations, and in civil society having the information to target those who do not. The tactic can have a big impact and may lead on to formal agreement through Track One diplomatic workings.

Different types of diplomacy are useful in different situations. As world population expands and Western-style profligacy continues, natural resources are stretched. For example, water supply is increasingly sparking tensions and disputes requiring negotiated solutions. One current example of Track Two diplomacy is of scientists and academics from mutually hostile countries, India and Pakistan, working together. One of the participants is the Professor of Pediatrics from the Aga Khan University Hospital in Karachi. He is convinced that the experience of working with Indian colleagues on issues such as the prevention of neo-natal deaths or stopping the spread of HIV/AIDS will create bonds which will survive international political changes and build peace between the two countries.

One stark problem remains though: governments which spend millions of dollars on arms are extremely reluctant to put any funds into preventing conflict. And the same goes for governments that supply arms to others.

The case of the Bolivian-Chile border dispute (see box) inspired a number of innovative proposals for solutions. Johan Galtung as a peace theorist proposed that the corridor of disputed land should belong to neither country but be made into an international nature preservation area. Mauricio Rios and Scott

---

The Bolivia-Chile challenge

In 1879, Chile seized 75,000 square miles of territory and 250 miles of coastline from Bolivia in a conflict known as the War of the Pacific. Ever since, Bolivians have fumed over the loss of the *Litoral de Atacama*, and their only access to the sea.

- In October 2003, opposition to the plans for exporting Bolivian gas through Chile helped spur a popular uprising which overthrew the elected President of Bolivia.
- His successor Carlos Mesa made the recovery of sovereign access to the Pacific his government's first foreign-policy priority.
- Trade talks with Chile have been cancelled. [Former] President Mesa said that further postponement of a solution to Bolivia's landlocked status could 'destabilize the region' because it 'has put Bolivian democracy at risk'.
- UN Secretary-General Kofi Annan, Mexican President Vicente Fox and former US President Jimmy Carter have volunteered assistance with mediation.
- The European Parliament, Venezuelan President Hugo Chavez, Argentinean President Nestor Kirchner and the Vatican have also offered assistance.

BUT
- Chilean officials deny they are hampering Bolivia's economic development.
- Chilean bureaucrats say the 1904 Treaty gives duty-free access to the northern Chilean port of Arica, which is linked by a Chilean funded rail-road to the Bolivian capital, La Paz.
- Chile wants to keep the issue bilateral (between the two countries) because international intervention would force them to negotiate.
- The Chilean President is said to need to conciliate the armed forces and the political right with maximal patriotism.
- Former US presidents Reagan and Carter supported Bolivia, current President George W Bush does not. ■

Source: James Langman *The Washington Times* 28 March 2004.

Working diplomatically

Fisher have proposed 'appreciative inquiry' as a tool for conflict resolution.[15] Appreciative inquiry is a technique for looking at the positive. It involves moving around a circle of the four Ds: discovery, dream, design and delivery to come up with new solutions. With yet another viewpoint, the Bolivian Trotskyist Faction has argued that what is needed is solidarity between the working classes of the two countries.

Certainly, disputes such as this one in which one party has every reason to seek change whilst the other party has an equally strong motivation to favor keeping things just the way they are, will be especially challenging since there is not even an agreement as to the need for opening preliminary talks. Similar situations are found where a strong national government sees no reason to negotiate with a group of secessionist rebels, as for example with France and the Corsicans and Spain with the Basques.

'Disaster diplomacy'

The most recent form of preventive diplomacy is 'disaster diplomacy' (yes, really). The idea is that disaster can act as a catalyst since the enormity of catastrophe changes people's perspectives and priorities and makes them willing to compromise and to try out new ways of doing things. Examples of where this has had an impact through mutual humanitarian gestures after the event include the 1999 earthquakes in Greece and Turkey; a series of hurricanes linking the US and Cuba and the 1991 to 1993 droughts in Africa.

A particularly good example is the Gujarat earthquake in 2001 which after a rocky start – India turned down Pakistan's offer of sniffer dogs to help find survivors – led to closer relations as India gratefully accepted Pakistani tents and blankets and both sides learnt the nuances of dialogue. Disaster, or the threat of disaster, can provide opportunities for enhancing collaboration among states but either the diplomacy must be between enemies facing a common danger (such as a drought or a flood) or be between those countries affected by the disaster and unaffected countries wishing to help, which can raise issues about the universality of humanitarian responses if help is only to be supplied to match diplomatic moves.

The US Government's belief in disaster diplomacy was evident in its reaction to the December 2004 tsunami, which killed more than 200,000 people in a dozen countries. However the level of US assistance after the waves was measured against the strategic importance of the countries affected. It would be good to see US disaster diplomacy spread to North Korea – constantly suffering from floods and droughts which then lead to famine because of its already ruined economy.

Again, without wishing a natural disaster on them, China and Taiwan could come closer through the experience of working together on a common, re-constructive program.

Experience shows that disaster and environmental management, international development and international relations are strongly linked, so all need to be taken into account when looking at how to minimize conflict within a region. No-one wishes for catastrophe but, once it has occurred, all tracks of diplomacy should attempt to extract as much positive impact as possible.

Means and ends

It is often said that diplomacy does not address the root causes of conflicts. This is true but whilst addressing root causes takes time, the killing is happening right now, and will carry on tomorrow and the next day, and the next. This is why any interventions that stop the fighting, even temporarily and however superficial they may be, are worth pursuing. In peacemaking as in life it can be a mistake to let the pursuit of the best possible outcome stand in the way of achieving a reasonable state of affairs.

'Structural violence' is the peace-builders' term for the daily experience of those who are discriminated against and kept in poverty, illiteracy and ill health. From one perspective it is true that real peace will not be achieved until justice is attained and structural violence ceases. But from the perspective of the poorest individuals and the poorest countries, they might rather be poor in an atmosphere of calm than poor and subject to ravaging bands of government troops or rebels ready and willing to kill, rape and maim them or take their children as soldiers. Diplomacy is very practical and works at the tasks to hand, from direct endeavors to stop cross-border incursions in the Great Lakes Region of Africa or piracy in the China Seas, to working to create international accepted norms to end the use of land mines and the recruitment of child soldiers.

1 Calculations made by Jonathan Freedland in 'Ten Steps to Peace', *The Guardian* 8 August 2001. See also 'The Lesser Unpleasantries of the Twentieth Century' website http://users.erols.com/mwhite28/warstat5.htm for a range of estimates of annual death tolls. **2** For information on genocide see http://www.preventgenocide.org/law/convention/text.htm **3** V Tishkov *Chechnya, Life in a War-Torn Society* (University of California Press 2004). **4** The World Bank has sponsored research on this issue (although with sometimes bizarre economic explanations) See www.worldbank.org/research/conflict/papers/greedand-grievance.htm **5** M Lund 'Underrating preventive diplomacy' *Foreign Affairs*, July 1995. **6** W Schneidman *Engaging Africa: Washington and the Fall of Portugal's Colonial Empire* (University Press of America 2004). **7** I Rabinovich *Waging Peace: Israel and the Arabs, 1948-2003* (Princeton University Press 2004). **8** S Touval 'Case Study: Lessons of Preventive Diplomacy in Yugoslavia' in C Crocker et al eds *Managing Global Chaos* (USIP Press 1996) p 403-418. **9** Former dictators' wealth is a good example of an issue requiring more honesty on the part of the Western countries, where such wealth is usually stored. Often the in-coming government is not keen on holding too rigorous a survey of the opportunities for presidential theft. **10** A George *Forceful Persuasion: Coercive Diplomacy as an Alternative to War* (USIP Press 1991) p 4. **11** M Anderson *Do No Harm: How aid can support peace or war* (Lynne Rienner 1999). **12** J McDonald 'Further explanations of track two diplomacy' in *Timing the De-Escalation of International Conflicts* Eds. Kriesberg and Thorson (Syracuse University Press 1991) pp 201-220. **13** www.iansa.org/ **14** www.monitor.upeace.org/archive.cfm?id_article=48 **15** M Rios and S Fisher 'Appreciative inquiry as a tool for conflict resolution' in C Sampson et al eds *Positive Approaches to Peace-building* (Pact Publications 2003) pp 237-256.

5 The UN, Darfur and oil-deals in Beijing

Largely neglected during the Cold War, UN peace-keeping has moved on from policing existing peace agreements to the much more ambitious task of trying to create peace where there is none.

IF TWO GANGS start shooting at each other in the street we expect the police to step in and stop the fighting. If two countries' armies start firing we now expect the UN to get agreement on a ceasefire and send in a peacekeeping force. But this is a relatively recent trend – before World War Two there was no UN. Between the two World Wars there was the League of Nations but this was a toothless tiger, debating railway gauges while Hitler invaded Poland.

Before the First World War there was nothing in any way equivalent to a global police force and the only hope for external intervention would have been for some more powerful government to bring pressure to bear on the two warring states to stop fighting. Certainly, the colonial powers often justified their interventions as keeping peace between warring groups (as in the *Pax Britannica* which was an imperial goal long before it became a board game). Indeed, before the horrors of the trench warfare of World War One, many men glorified war and despised peace.

Scourge of war

The UN's primary mission, as defined immediately after the Second World War, is 'to save succeeding

---

'War is the foundation of all high virtues and faculties of men.'
John Ruskin (1819-1900), artist and critic.

'Perpetual peace is a dream, and it is not even a beautiful dream.'
Field-Marshal Helmuth Von Moltke (1800-1891), Prussian General. ∎

generations from the scourge of war'. Yet from the start the UN has suffered from 'a dual and conflicting mandate': it is supposed to act on the best interests of *all* the world's peoples whilst respecting the sovereignty of individual nations and not interfering in their internal affairs. Until very recently the UN had to stand by when governments chose to massacre their own citizens. Even had the UN Charter been in place at the time, Hitler could not have been prevented from launching the holocaust against German Jews and other minorities but only from invading Poland. Poland was an international matter – killing six million national citizens was not.

As current UN Secretary-General Kofi Annan has correctly claimed, the UN invented both the word and the concept of peacekeeping. However, it did so only by improvising in respect to specific situations and events. The foundation concept was that nations would bring their disputes to the UN, where they would be resolved by discussion, including the good offices of neighbors and other countries with an interest in the resolution of the issues. This was however an excessively civilized view of conflicts between nations, which are often brutal power struggles prolonged by leaders who continue to put their personal interests before the welfare of their peoples.

Peace operations
UN peacekeeping originally meant the deployment of military forces to act as a barrier to ensure the maintenance of an agreed truce between hostile parties

---

Sinai: UN's first peacekeeping mission
Peacekeeping in the modern sense did not exist until 1956. This was when the UN sent a force to the Sinai Peninsula to monitor the withdrawal of British, French and Israeli forces from Egypt, which they had invaded after the nationalization of the Suez Canal. The UN forces kept the peace for 10 years until 1967 when they were expelled by Egypt, leading to an immediate resumption of war. ∎

– no truce, no peacekeepers. This simple mandate has now evolved into more complex multiple goals which include the political, social and economic restructuring of war-torn states. 'Peace operations' is now the preferred term since it covers a much broader range of activities – including creating peace in countries with on-going internal wars and longer-term peace-building.

Peacekeeping missions are approved by a 'Chapter VI mandate' vote in the UN which generally provides for soldiers to keep an already agreed peace by standing between the two sides, often policing a neutral zone. Now, however, peacekeeping is often enlarged into actual peace *enforcement* where fighting between the parties is still continuing and the UN soldiers in their blue helmets are allowed to use all measures necessary under their 'rules of engagement', which define when UN soldiers are actually allowed to fire their weapons (a Chapter VII mandate).

The peace operations in Burundi, Bosnia and Somalia have all involved peace enforcement as did Operation Desert Storm (1991) in the Gulf, which was a response to an inter-state conflict between Iraq and Kuwait. UN peace enforcement is always problematic because there is an unreal expectation that none of the UN forces will be killed nor be required to kill anyone else. The hope is that the threat of mass force will be enough to make hostile governments and rampaging warriors back off.

UN constraints

The UN is not a world government.[1] Under its Charter it can only do what its member countries collectively allow it to do.[2] Throughout the Cold War the UN was a 'world-class metaphor for hopeless paralysis', to quote its supporters in the US United Nations Association, since it could not act unless both East and West were in agreement. The involvement in Korea (1950-53) only happened because the USSR was boycotting the UN at the time. Even where there was agreement on a desirable outcome, the Communist states were opposed to any internal intervention, which might set a precedent at home.

Even today, China and Russia still oppose intervention to prevent genocide in Darfur, Sudan, because of their own sensitivities over potential interference in Tibet and Chechnya. The advantage of the UN over bodies such as the World Bank and the International Monetary Fund (IMF), where votes depend on financial shares, is that in the UN's Parliament (the General Assembly) each country, however big or small, has one vote. This is hard on the one billion citizens of China or the 800 millions of India but good for the 12,000 of Tuvalu. In reality, even in the looking-glass world of the UN, size does count for something – as does budget contribution – but the developing countries, if they act together, are in the majority.

The 'ministerial cabinet' of the UN (The Security Council) is made up of five permanent members: China, France, Russia, the UK and the US. Each of these has an individual veto. In addition, 10 members are elected by the General Assembly for two-year terms and are veto-less. Israel, which can often only summon up four or five supporting votes in the General Assembly, survives at the UN because of US backing and use of its veto in the Security Council. This is why, say, the posting of a UN peacekeeping force between Israel and Palestine is unthinkable: it would be vetoed by the US.

Since the Cold War there have been many proposals for reform, but no-one realistically expects the Security Council's five permanent members to relinquish their vetoes – and no one can force them to do so. One interesting reform proposal that combines representation with peacemaking is to offer India a permanent seat (without veto) on the Security

Council, conditional on its reaching a final agreement with Pakistan over Kashmir. In an age where the new 'iron curtain', to quote President Musharraf of Pakistan, is descending between Muslims and non-Muslims, there is currently no Muslim Permanent Member, nor indeed any African or Latin American to represent their regions' interests.

Who wears the blue helmets?

The UN has no soldiers of its own. Most peacekeeping missions are carried out by a fruit-salad of assorted national troops provided by member countries to act under the auspices of the UN and the command of a spare general from a country prepared to put up a lot of troops. They wear blue helmets so that they stand out in the field.

The current UN Mission in Liberia (UNMIL), for example, which is faced with the task of stopping brothers from killing each other, consists of 15,000 troops from 47 nations.[3] Creating a functional force from such disparate elements demands an outstanding level of management and co-ordination. Individual nations can also be subcontractors for a peacekeeping mission such as the French in Rwanda, the Russians in Georgia, and NATO members in Bosnia and Kosovo. The establishment of the multi-country International Security Assistance Force (ISAF) in Afghanistan in 2002, was authorized by the UN although it is not officially a UN peacekeeping body. UN Missions are spread around the world.

How big are we talking?

Opponents of the UN present its Secretariat as a vast, sprawling bureaucracy. However the professional staff of the Secretariat in New York totals 3,200 – comparable to the 3,500 staff of the General Accounts Office of the US Congress. Total Secretariat staff, including back-up personnel such as computer programmers,

Blue helmets

Below are the UN peacekeeping, observer and enforcement missions, in 2003. As of December 2003 the five largest contributors of personnel to UN peacekeeping operations provided 43 per cent of all military and civilian police forces. These countries in descending order were Pakistan, Bangladesh, Nigeria, India and Ghana. The 19 NATO member countries, whose combined defense expenditures exceed 60 per cent of the global total, provided only 9 per cent of all UN peacekeeping personnel at the end of 2003. The largest NATO contributor was Poland which in committing 735 military and civilian police personnel was ranked 15th in the list of UN contributors.

- MINUCI (UN Mission in Cote d'Ivoire)*
- MINURSO (UN Mission for the Referendum in Western Sahara)
- MONUC (UN Organization Mission in the Democratic Republic of Congo)
- UNAMA (UN Assistance Mission in Afghanistan)
- UNAMSIL (UN Mission in Sierra Leone)
- UNDOF (UN Disengagement Observer Force): Israel, Syria
- UNFICYP (UN Peacekeeping Force in Cyprus)
- UNIFIL (UN Interim Force in Lebanon)
- UNIKOM (UN Iraq-Kuwait Observation Mission)**
- UNMA (UN Mission in Angola)**

- UNMEE (UN Mission in Ethiopia and Eritrea)
- UNMIK (UN Interim Administration Mission in Kosovo)
- UNMIL (UN Mission in Liberia)*
- UNMISET (UN Mission of Support in Timor Leste/East Timor)
- UNMOGIP (UN Military Observer Group in India and Pakistan)
- UNOMIG (UN Observer Mission in Georgia)
- UNTSO (UN Truce Supervision Organization): Egypt, Lebanon, Syria

* Mission started 2003 ** Mission ended 2003

Other organizations are also involved in such work – for example the Organization of American States (OAS) has a mission to Haiti; the Organization for Security and Co-operation in Europe (OCSE) has missions in Chechnya, Bosnia, and Kosovo among other places. There is the African Mission to Burundi (AMIB), and RAMSI, the Regional Assistance Mission to the Solomon Islands.

Major sources: UN reports; OSCE reports; Canadian Department of National Defence; Ploughshares conflicts database

comes to 9,000 – less than the 9,900 running the Canadian city of Winnipeg.

The total of all UN personnel around the world including agencies such as the UN High Commissioner for Refugees (UNHCR), the Food and Agriculture Organization (FAO) and the UN Children's Fund (UNICEF) is 51,500. These people, from drivers to directors, are engaged in political, economic and social affairs, industry, education, labor and employment, development, refugees, human rights, civil aviation, agriculture, health, children, population, world weather services, telecommunications, postal services, international maritime co-operation, intellectual property, atomic energy and yet more. The 50,000 is hardly a large number to cover such a range of tasks globally, especially when there are 10,000 people making and advertising Coca-Cola in Thailand alone.

Despite all the barriers to action, including the increasing reluctance of the West to put its troops at risk, the UN is still heavily engaged in peacekeeping on the ground across the globe. As of the end of 2004, there were 17 such UN operations in the field with a total of 70,000 troops. This total contrasts with the US, which has more than 150,000 troops just in Iraq.[4]

The price of peace

As with so many other potential activities in support of peace, one of the greatest constraints upon the UN's role is a simple lack of finance. Even if they are not fighting, keeping troops in the field is very expensive. In 2001 the UN's annual budget for 14 peacekeeping operations was $2,740 million (in comparison, the Australian annual defense budget was $18,000 million for protecting 20 million people). All of the UN's peace operations in a year generally cost less than the annual peacetime costs for two US army divisions.

In 2001 the most expensive activity was $700 million for keeping the peace in war-torn Sierra

The UN, Darfur and oil-deals in Beijing

Leone and the least expensive was $6 million for the Military Observer Group watching the nuclear states of India and Pakistan. Any kind of economic analysis will show that keeping the peace is much cheaper than prosecuting a war but once politics enters the debate even the best economic arguments fail. Since, commensurate with the size of its economy, the US is allocated the biggest share of funding for UN peace-keeping activities and because the US is campaigning for China and Russia to pay a bigger share, humanitarian interventions to save hundreds of thousands of lives stall while bean-counters debate who is to pay what.

There have been a number of proposals for the UN to have its own standing army, trained for peacekeeping not fighting, ready to go into the field. Whilst finance would be a major hurdle, an even bigger issue would be the power this would give to the UN Secretary-General as commander-in-chief. A proposal with a greater chance of success would be for individual countries to keep some national troops and police ready for dispatch (as Fiji already does).

New world order

The end of the Cold War era in 1989 brought both an increased demand for peacekeeping operations and a greater sophistication in what they were being asked to do. From 1948 to1988 there had only been 15 such UN operations and just 3 of these went beyond peace monitoring. By contrast, from 1989 to 1991 there were 31 UN peace missions, 24 of which were of a highly complex nature.

For example, the mission for the decolonization of South West Africa into the independent state of Namibia (UNTAG) in 1989 was the first to monitor democratic elections, a task which has since become commonplace. It was also typical of the monitoring of agreed stand-offs, in that more UN soldiers died in road accidents, speeding in their tax-free sports cars, than in keeping the peace.

The Cambodian mission (UNTAC) in 1992-93 was the most extensive and successful UN mission ever, since it succeeded in bringing a large nation back from internal genocide to democratic elections. The political, social and economic construction of Timor Leste/East Timor under UNTAET is another example of the UN being able to act as the midwife at the (re) birth of a nation. In both cases success depended on there being developed countries that were ready to provide massive financial support, and the local neighbors deciding to cease their internal meddling because of broader changes in the regional geopolitical situation.

In West Africa by contrast, with missions such as UNMIL in Liberia and UNAMSIL in Sierra Leone, Europe and the US have limited interest or staying power in funding the exercise and warriors; guns and illicit goods continue to cross highly porous international borders, so that warfare is constantly erupting. It is the tragedy of these new wars that the guns are in the hands of those with an interest in continuing the fighting and that the women, children and men who only want to live a normal life, planting their crops or going to school, are voiceless and without power.[5]

UN 'Peacekeeping activities' now often include 'humanitarian intervention' as in Somalia in 1992. The complex mandate has become standard for the 'second-generation' peacekeeping missions where the emphasis is on reconstruction and peace implementation rather than the conflict-freezing of the 'first generation'. The UN is now charged with trying to put Humpty Dumpty back together again by rebuilding failed nations.

Always reasons to fight

Today, most conflict is no longer about ideology. The East-West stand-offs are over and most fighting is inside rather than between states. Many of these clashes are based on racial or ethnic tensions which resurrect historical grievances – such as the battles in former Yugoslavia. Such wars are exceedingly difficult to mediate, either because no one is in control or because those who are in control can only maintain their positions by inflaming ethnic stereotypes which demonize the opposition.

In a war between nations, it becomes permissible for the protagonists to hate each other and regard the opposition as de-personalized sub-humans (remember the US troops being trained to think of the North Vietnamese as 'gooks'?). In a civil war, or in that cruel chaos that afflicts many African countries, if the fighting is to cease forever, then people cannot just go home and sit on either side of a geographical border. The Israel/Palestine issue is so difficult

---

Child soldier in Guatemala

E was recruited into the Guatemalan army (the civil war lasting over 20 years began in 1968) when he was 14. 'The army was a nightmare. We suffered greatly from the cruel treatment we received. We were constantly beaten, mostly for no reason at all, just to keep us in a state of terror. I still have a scar on my lip and sharp pains in my stomach from being brutally kicked by the older soldiers. The food was scarce, and they made us walk with heavy loads, much too heavy for our small and malnourished bodies. They forced me to learn how to fight the enemy, in a war that I didn't understand why it was being fought.' ∎

Source: Peace Pledge Union

---

precisely because the Palestinians do not yet have a viable country within whose national borders they can withdraw.

After civil strife, people have to learn to restore their relationships with their neighbors and communities, to deal peacefully with one another and work democratically. This can only come about if each one accepts that everyone else is also a person with the same human rights. Imagine trying to achieve this after members of your family have been hacked to death, as in Rwanda in 1994's genocide. But it can be, and has been done. As a Rwandan bishop commented, 'I have shaken the hand of the man who murdered my father – nothing after that will ever be as difficult again.'

Blue helmets no longer enough

The internationalization of terrorism across borders and links between the global economy and civil wars has greatly expanded the concept of security. For the UN the simple freezing of conflict across national borders has evolved into reconstruction of entire political, social and economic systems. Peacekeepers now require a whole range of skills in peacemaking and constructing peace. No longer are blue helmets, discipline and shiny guns enough.[6] Missions to keep the peace need to have a shared strategic analysis of what is going on, to secure people's involvement from the start so that the community knows that it is responsible for its own reconstruction; and to create good military-civilian collaboration.

Body counts

In today's world, when actual fighting rather than standing guard is required, the Security Council mandates NATO (as in the Balkans in 1999), or fails to mandate a 'coalition of the willing' as in Iraq in 2003. The 'mandate to NATO' solution may well be the answer in Europe but does not resolve the question

'We now see, with chilling clarity, that a world where many millions of people endure brutal oppression and extreme misery will never be fully secure, even for its most privileged inhabitants.' *Kofi Annan* (1938-), UN Secretary-General. ∎

of what is to happen in Africa, where there is no equivalent of NATO, and yet is the location of most current and potential conflicts.

The African Union (AU) can provide troops of varying levels of training and discipline, but it cannot afford to keep them in the field without outside sponsorship. The unfortunate reality is that the resources for peacekeeping are generally found in those regions which least need them, which is why it is essential to have a global rather than a regional approach. Even at the UN – or at its heart, the Security Council – a form of racism is evident in the political impact of the body count: 1,000,000 deaths in Africa (Rwanda/DR Congo/Sudan) do not have the same impact as 10,000 in Europe (former Yugoslavia) or 4,000 fatalities in America (9/11). At a time when $5 million a day was being spent on Yugoslavia the Security Council refused the Secretary-General $5 million for a year's expenditure in Liberia. In any score-sheet of the UN's successes and failures in peacekeeping and resolving conflict this calculus of concern has to be kept in mind (see box *Score card for the UN*). At the meeting where he discussed Rwanda with former UN Secretary-General Boutros Boutros-Ghali, President Clinton spent most of the time ensuring that an American would be appointed to head up UNICEF. The bosses in the UN, the Permanent Members of the Security Council, have a much greater interest for good or evil in countries which have substantial oil reserves.

Interventions

In recent years, the Security Council has authorized military interventions in states unable to prevent a humanitarian catastrophe (Somalia); following the deposition of an elected head of government (Haiti) and in the wake of economic collapse and social disorder (Albania).[7] UN successes have included Namibia, Mozambique, El Salvador and Timor Leste/East Timor. The lesson to be learnt from the failures such as Angola and Somalia is that no UN force should be sent in to keep a peace that does not exist, nor one to which the parties themselves show no commitment. The critical factor now is for standards governing the use of force by non-state actors to be strengthened and for UN member governments to work out ways of enforcing them. Disturbing as the idea is of states such as Iran or North Korea having nuclear weapons, the prospect of terrorists with such devices is beyond horror. There are already 12 international terrorism conventions – but no real consensus as to who are the terrorists since my terrorist is your freedom fighter and visa versa.

'I used to lie on the floor on my stomach to avoid the bullets whilst I was doing my homework. I never wanted to have my 12th birthday because at 12 you have to join the army.' *Oscar Torres* from El Salvador, maker of the film Innocent Voices based on his own experience as a child-soldier. ∎

The 2000 Report of the Panel on United Nations Peace Operations (Brahimi Report) argued that 'the consent of the local parties, impartiality and the use of force only in self-defense should remain the bedrock principles of peacekeeping'.[8] Yet this is unrealistic – where one party to a peace agreement clearly and incontrovertibly is violating its terms, continued equal treatment of all parties by the UN at best-results in ineffectiveness and at worst amounts to complicity with evil. No failure did more to damage the standing and credibility of UN peacekeeping in the 1990s than its reluctance to distinguish victim from aggressor, as

The UN, Darfur and oil-deals in Beijing

Score card for the UN

The UN has a mixed record when it comes to resolving conflict – but other players such as the permanent members of the Security Council have a large influence over what the UN can do.

SUCCESSES

172 Peace Settlements
- Ending Iran-Iraq War 1988-91
- Ending civil war in El Salvador 1991-95
- Soviet troop withdrawal from Afghanistan 1988-90
- Namibia* 1989-90
- Cambodia* 1991-93
- Mozambique* 1992-94
- Tajikistan* 1994-2000
- Macedonia 1995-99
- Timor Leste/East Timor* 1999-2005

FAILURES
- Somalia 1992-93, 1993-95 [Ignominious withdrawal]
- Rwanda 1993-96 [1994 genocide]
- Bosnia 1993-95 [1995 Srebrenica massacre]
- Angola 1989-1997 [Continuing fighting]
- Sierra Leone 1999-present [Rebels kidnapped UN peacekeepers]
- Haiti 2004-present [Chaos: rich benefit/poor suffer]

TOO EARLY TO JUDGE

Kosovo, Afghanistan*, Sudan – Darfur, DR Congo

* Areas where elements of nation-building were added to peacekeeping.

for example in Rwanda, Bosnia and Kosovo.

UN troops have to be able to defend themselves. So plans for dealing with lawless rebels must be based on the worst expectations, and use larger, better-equipped forces with superior intelligence information. Even more vitally, UN peacekeepers – troops or police – who witness violence against civilians should be presumed to be authorized to stop it, in support of basic humanitarian principles and universal human rights. The UN Secretariat must be bold in telling the Security Council what it needs to know, not what it wants to hear, when recommending resource levels for a new mission. Those levels have to be set according to realistic scenarios that take into account likely challenges to implementation.

UN peacekeeping has a checkered career. However

in order to judge we need to have a clear idea of what constitutes success. The simplest measure is a body count – how many people were killed and how many people were saved from being killed. Counting the dead is easiest – it is always more difficult to know how many people would have been killed without UN intervention and how long their reprieve will last. There is agreement that Rwanda and Bosnia were failures because the UN stood by whilst so many died. Somalia was more of a loss of face – the UN went in but withdrew without achieving peace. Sadly successes receive less fanfare than failures. And the more complex the UN mandate, the harder it is to give the mission as a whole a simple pass or a fail. Peacekeepers today are expected to provide the space for peace agreements to take root. They can enable refugees and internally displaced people to go home. Disarming combatants and reintegrating them into civil society is another role. Peacekeepers can offer citizens a chance to live without the fear of being caught in crossfire. They can also bring war criminals to justice and assist national leaders to build democratic institutions. To call any UN mission a 'success' invites derision from the critics. And even the UN's friends continually call for more impact and more sensitivity to local wishes. And of course, labeling something a 'success' too early is risky since there is almost always the potential

---

Dallaire's stand in Rwanda

General Romeo Dallaire was the Canadian in charge of the UN forces in Rwanda as the massacres started in April 1994. The UN Secretary-General Boutros Boutros-Ghali told him to withdraw. His reply:

'"I can't, I've got thousands [of people to protect] in areas under our control…" The situation was going to shit… And, I said, "No, I can't leave".'

He is still traumatized by the experience. ∎

Source: *Amnesty International Magazine* Winter 2002.

for fighting to break out once more, as in Angola throughout the 1990s.

Why doesn't the UN prevent genocide?

UN Secretary-General Boutros Boutros-Ghali was not being callous when he ordered UN troops out of Rwanda in 1994 as the massacres raged on. He was a public servant who did not have the permission of his bosses to save lives[9], although many argue that both he and Kofi Annan (then head of UN peacekeeping) could have done more to prevent the killing. Annan said at the 10 years' memorial 'I realised after the genocide that there was more that I could and should have done to sound the alarm and rally support.'

Genocide is an unforgivable crime. It is also one crime the international community agrees should be subject to international control. Yet the last thing that a state which is prepared to massacre its own citizens will accept is interference from outside to stop the killing. The 20th century was the bloodiest in human history, millions died in battles, but even more – estimates vary between 60 to 150 millions – were innocent victims of genocide and mass slaughter by their own governments.[10] Stalin killed more Russians than Hitler did.

The debate continues as to how far genocide occurs because of mass feelings or because of manipulative leaders: would there have been a holocaust without Hitler, or Cambodia's killing fields without Pol Pot? If the leaders are the instigators and the mass killings are not inevitable consequence of evils deeply rooted

---

Wise too late after the event

'For us, genocide was the gas chamber, what happened in Germany. We were not able to realize that with the machete you can create genocide. Later, we understood this.' *Boutros Boutros-Ghali* (1922-), Former UN Secretary-General, speaking about Rwanda, on PBS Radio 21 January 2004. ∎

in society but rather the outcome of state violence, then the UN, with the support of member states, is more likely to be able to stop genocide and thus has a greater moral responsibility to do so.

Where the UN fails to stop genocide it is because the member countries (and more particularly the Security Council which has the final say) lack the political will to act and thus to move fast to back the UN and provide troops and finance in situations where time is critical. In the current crisis in Darfur, Sudan, where 70,000 civilians have been killed and 1.8 million uprooted under the sponsorship of their national government, no country is volunteering to lead in a UN force to stop the carnage. Furthermore, Security Council members China and Russia who both have sensitivities at home and oil and arms deals with the Sudanese Government, are actively opposing UN action.

Bougainville

The peacekeeping/peace-monitoring force on the island of Bougainville in the South Pacific has been hailed as a successful example of a model developed outside the UN system. A regional force of troops from Australia, New Zealand/Aotearoa, Fiji and Vanuatu went into Bougainville after a decade of vicious civil war. The monitoring group included civilians and women. One of the key factors was that the communities had fellow Pacific islanders and civilians working with them. This facilitated reconciliation as monitors worked directly with local peace committees and clan leaders. As one of the former rebels commented, 'When we saw that the Australians were bringing their women here, we knew that they were serious – they wouldn't have done that unless they were sure that they were going to create peace.'

In Africa, as in the Pacific, the future may well involve more regional peacekeeping and fewer UN grab bags of culturally ill-matched troops with little knowledge of the local scene. On the other hand, there will always be a place for outsiders who are clearly neutral *because* they have no particular interest in the region. Fijians have been highly successful as peace-keepers in the Middle East and the Balkans for that very reason: they have come in as outsiders. Ninety per cent of peacekeeping is about establishing and maintaining trust and there can be few rules about trust. As French author Balzac said, 'you don't have to like your banker, you just have to trust him' and the same is true of peacekeepers.

'What a dump – how long are we going to be here?'

The task of peacekeeping – stopping the gunfire – can be accomplished much more quickly than the work of peace-building which requires the reconstruction of services and institutions and links between people. Often the UN mission, limited to two to three years for financial and military deployment reasons, is ended before the peace-building aims have been realized. Given the different time-frames involved, the UN may need to separate military and civilian mandates for peace-building.

In the Solomon Islands, for example, the Australian Government always made it clear that military and civilian assistance would be provided on separate timetables and for as long as required to rebuild the country. Since the Solomons is a group of islands and ethnic groups thrown together into nationhood by a colonial whim, many institutions will not just need to be rebuilt; they will need to be developed from scratch and people will need be given the time and training to make them work. In the end, the continuance of peace there depends on being able to create sustainable economic growth at a rate fast enough to keep pace with population growth, so that there are opportunities for young people who are no longer satisfied with traditional subsistence life-styles.[11]

Role of civil society

There are currently over 40,000 multilateral treaties registered with the UN. There is a mass of paperwork, and too much of it deals with trade rather than defense. Although the razzmatazz of dispatching the blue helmets off to another war zone makes for exciting TV news, the less glamorous, less visible foot-slog of creating treaties – such as banning the use of land-mines and controlling the sale of small arms – will have a far greater impact on the lives of war-weary peasant farmers in the Majority World. 'Rogue states' and militia bands inside failed states may ignore treaties, but they are still dependent on other countries to sell them arms or buy their diamonds or oil.[12] Here, treaties can work by maximizing the pressure on the outside partners (who are often transnational firms) to observe international standards in the treaties signed by their governments.

Civil society can change the fate of small countries through boycotts and lobbying of companies whose behavior is unacceptable if not actually illegal. Far more needs to be done to name and shame the bad guys who have oil deals with genocidal governments or sell arms to rebels that recruit child soldiers at gunpoint. It is no accident that four of the five permanent members of the Security Council are amongst the world's leading arms dealers.

UN-less world?

Because the current situation is so unsatisfactory, many argue for radical change, with the following three main options:

1 Abolish the UN and then either welcome the imposition of *Pax Americana* across the world or accept living with a state of anarchy between countries.
2 Continue with the UN, greatly reformed.

Men into the mud

You may fly over a land forever; you may bomb it, atomize it, pulverize it and wipe it clean of life. But if you desire to defend it, protect it, and keep it for civilization, you must do this on the ground, the way the Roman legions did, by putting your young men into the mud. ■

Source: From retired Colonel TR Fehrenbach's book on Korea, *This Kind of War*. It is now on the US Army's official reading list.

---

3 Work towards some form of world federation or world government.

Amongst supporters of the UN there is a division of opinion between those who believe that all that is needed is for members, most particularly the US, to summon up the political will to make the system work and those who argue the need for root and branch reform. Since we do not currently have a world-wide voting system (although this could be possible through the internet) we do not know which option the peoples of the world would choose. In most countries, including the US, the general public has very little idea of how the UN works, and even less information on possible alternatives. Recent debates over acceptance of the new constitution for the European Union (EU) show just how distrustful the public are of supra-national organizations whose workings they do not understand.

However, if the UN were to be abolished today, by next week many smaller and middle-sized countries would already be proposing to replace it with something very similar.

Currently the US uses the UN when it suits and ignores it when it is inconvenient. But as the balance of world power inevitably shifts, the rising powers such as China, India or the EU will be able to pressure the US increasingly to acknowledge the utility of the UN.

There are other options. Writer George Monbiot, in his credo *The Age of Consent: A Manifesto for a New World Order*, has proposed that the UN be replaced by a genuinely democratic world parliament. However, optimistic as he is, Monbiot does not see such a Parliament exercising more than 'moral force' on international opinion, since he recognizes that states are still responsible for waging war and controlling internal violence.

For the time being, then, it seems that the UN with all its flaws is our only option.

1 See L Polman (translated R Black) *We did nothing: why the truth doesn't always come out when the UN goes in* (Penguin 2003). **2** The UN Charter is at www.un.org/aboutun/charter/ **3** UNMIL 2003 online, http://www.un.org **4** See http://www.diggerhistory.info/pages-medals/un1.htm **5** M Berdal, 'How 'new' are 'new' wars? Global economic change and the study of civil war', *Global Governance*, October 2003. **6** See J Galtung 'Cultural Violence', *Journal of Peace Research*, Vol 27, No 3, 1990 pp 291-305; JP Lederach, Building Peace. *Sustainable Reconciliation in Divided Societies*, Washington DC: United States Institute of Peace Press, 1997; C Mitchell 'Necessitous Man and Conflict Resolution: More Basic Questions About Human Needs Theory', in J Burton (ed) *Conflict Human Needs Theory*, (Macmillan 1990) pp 149-176. **7** S Chesterman et al *Making States Work: From State Failure to State-Building* (International Peace Academy: New York 2004). **8** Official *Report of the Panel on UN Peace Operations*, United Nations 2000. **9** M Barnett *Eyewitness to a Genocide: the United Nations and Rwanda* (Cornell University Press 2002). **10** B Valentino, *Final Solutions: Mass Killing and Genocide in the 20th Century* (Cornell University Press 2004). **11** H Ware 'Demography, migration and conflict in the Pacific' *Journal of Peace Research* 42(4): 437-457, 2005. **12** Berdal (note 5) describes how this worked in Angola.

6 The costs of war

The human, environmental and economic costs of war are so great that it is hard to see why people ever choose to fight. Death tolls are only one element. Life for the 'survivors', often maimed, widowed, or former child soldiers, is harsh. On top come the dollar costs measured in billions.

IN OUR TOPSY-TURVY world we spend huge amounts of money on men and mortars, yet very little to prevent bloodshed. No-one doubts that preventing war is vastly cheaper than mopping up afterwards. Yet to date the world has not been able to devise a political – or should that be economic? – system which favors peace. The current pattern of sovereign nation states enables fighting between them but does not make prevention of war a common goal. The EU is in an experiment in a new system beyond the nation state which has yet to be tried in other regions. Within nations War Offices may have become Ministries of Defense but Departments of Peace are still only a dream.[1]

In families, severe discord causes trauma and can reduce both well-being and income. At the work-place, employers recognize that the monetary costs of conflict are high enough to make it well worth paying for staff training in how to handle conflict: witness the mass of advertisements on the web for fee-paying courses on 'conflict resolution in the workplace'. In some societies where there is little overt violence, there is interest in keeping out of the

---

'Every gun that is made, every warship launched, every rocket fired signifies in the final sense, a theft from those who hunger and are not fed, those who are cold and are not clothed. This world in arms is not spending money alone. It is spending the sweat of its laborers, the genius of its scientists, the hopes of its children.' *Dwight D Eisenhower* (1890-1969), US General, later President. ■

courts, which require a winner and a loser, turning instead to conflict mediation which leaves all sides satisfied with the outcome.[2]

Too many deaths

The human and material costs of violent conflict are almost unimaginable. Death is the final cost, with its devastating and final impact. From 1900-1987 there were 34 million deaths in wars between states and an additional 169 million deaths in wars and conflicts inside sovereign states.[3] Beyond those who are directly killed in action by bombs, bullets or machetes are those who die from associated causes: diseases spread by war, the lack of health care, food, clean water and shelter.[4] Death is the ultimate disaster, and the impact of death reverberates outwards from the grieving family, where children are orphaned and there is no breadwinner, to societies that lose the flower of a whole generation. After the First World War all of Europe was traumatized by the experience, and the lack of dealing with the issues led on to the Second World War as those who had never recovered re-fought their old battles.

'I am afraid. I can no longer go through a tunnel or cross a bridge. In the tram I am sometimes dizzy, and I feel I want to kill myself or the other passengers. I am constantly haunted by visions of fighting. My mind is unstable and unwell, my life is ruined.' Sarajevo resident, 1999. ∎

Doing the sums

Poor countries are more likely to experience conflict and conflict makes countries poor. The costs of modern warfare rapidly reach numbers so large that they are difficult to comprehend. The Vietnam War (1960-75) cost some $111 billion at the time, or more than $500 billion in today's dollars. It also made it impossible for President Johnson to build the 'Great Society' in the US as he had planned. A significant

The costs of war

Human development and armed conflict

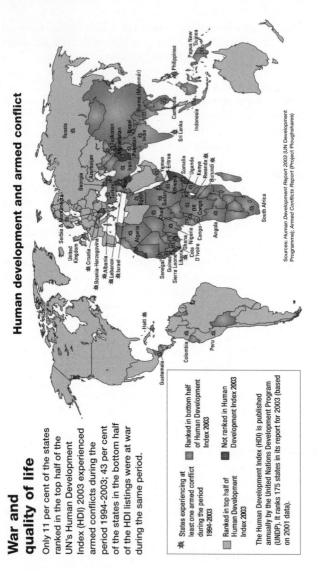

War and quality of life

Only 11 per cent of the states ranked in the top half of the UN's Human Development Index (HDI) 2003 experienced armed conflicts during the period 1994-2003; 43 per cent of the states in the bottom half of the HDI listings were at war during the same period.

Sources: *Human Development Report 2003* (UN Development Programme); *Armed Conflicts Report* (Project Ploughshares)

✷ States experiencing at least one armed conflict during the period 1994-2003

Ranked in top half of Human Development Index 2003

Ranked in bottom half of Human Development Index 2003

Not ranked in Human Development Index 2003

The Human Development Index (HDI) is published annually by the United Nations Development Program (UNDP). It ranks 175 states in its report for 2003 (based on 2001 data).

part of the US's costs of that war are still being paid out through the pensions for the Vietnam veterans and the families of those killed in the war. No-one has yet calculated the cost of the war to the Vietnamese.

For the 1980-88 Iran-Iraq war the estimated costs to Iran were $644 billion (including $450 billion in war damage) and $453 billion (including $67 billion in war damage) for Iraq. These totals are so high because of the estimates for lost oil-export income.

Sri Lanka's war since 1983, currently with a fragile ceasefire, is more typical of armed conflicts in the Majority World. In real terms, government military expenditure showed a five-fold increase between 1981 and 1991 rising from 0.7 to 3.4 per cent of GNP. The Government has been financing the conflict by post-poning expenditure on infrastructure items (sensible, as these are likely to be blown up). The impact on the economy as a whole seems to have been a reduction of about 10 per cent in economic growth. Over a 10-year period the country has lost the equivalent of about one year's total GDP (Gross Domestic Product).[5]

Twelve years of war in El Salvador reduced the national standard of living to half of what it had been before the war.[6] One study of 15 countries at war in the 1980s, when compared with more peaceful low-income countries, showed that strife is associated with slow if any growth, declining food production, declining export volumes and high inflation.[7] This is not surprising. There are also the costs of death and destruction: lives, families and homes, and services all have monetary as well as emotional costs. Then there are the costs of the lost alternatives. For example, if Sri Lanka had not been torn apart by war it could have been as rich as Malaysia is today. The costs to rich world countries are not insignificant either. Currently US families are paying an average of $500 a month for the 'War on Terror', half of it from taxes and the other half from borrowings against the future. Vietnam veterans in the US now have to pay a fee just to sign up for eligibility for a visit to a veterans' hospital and New York's emergency services are so underfunded that they could not handle another 9/11.

The cost of a single item of high-tech military equipment would pay for significant amounts of food or development. For the price of one fighter plane a country such as Zambia could buy quarter of a million tons of rice or put a third of a million children through primary school. Guns or butter is a real choice, or for the poorest the choice is guns or rice.

The environmental costs of war start well before the outbreak of hostilities, as resources are diverted from ecological protection to military spending. Earth, air and water suffer from pollution caused by arms production and the direct impacts of weapons-testing and military training. The military are notorious polluters who are exempted from environmental regulations. Soviet bases in the former East Germany polluted four per cent of the country's territory.

In the 1980s Ethiopia spent five times as much on fighting Eritrea and Tigre as it would have cost to reverse desertification by tree-planting and soil conservation – and thus to have avoided the 1985 famine which killed over a million people. From carpet bombing to landmines to 'scorched earth' campaigns that devastate the land so it cannot support life, war routinely ravages ecosystems and rips apart agricultural livelihoods. Scorched earth operations in Central America have obliterated vast areas of agricultural land and crucial ecosystems, pushing millions of refugees into city slums and overtaxed hillsides.[8]

Fantastic temperatures of 3,000° Celsius (5,432° Fahrenheit) are reached by a heavy bomb exploding. No flora and fauna can survive; but also the lower layers of soil are destroyed for the next 7,000 years. In the 1991 Gulf War oil pollution contaminated 20 per cent of mangroves, 50 per cent of coral reefs and

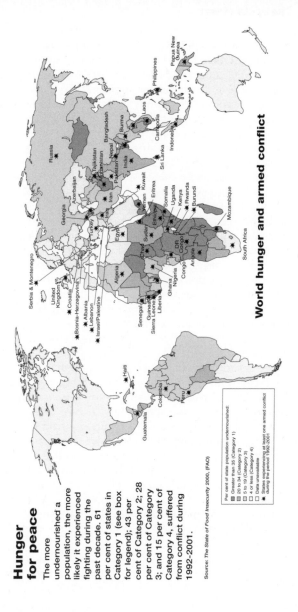

Hunger for peace

The more undernourished a population, the more likely it experienced fighting during the past decade. 61 per cent of states in Category 1 (see box for legend); 43 per cent of Category 2; 28 per cent of Category 3; and 15 per cent of Category 4, suffered from conflict during 1992-2001.

Source: *The State of Food Insecurity 2000*, (FAO)

World hunger and armed conflict

Per cent of state population undernourished:

- ▨ Greater than 35 (Category 1)
- ▨ 20 to 34 (Category 2)
- ☐ 5 to 19 (Category 3)
- ☐ 4 or less (Category 4)
- ☐ Data unavailable

✴ States experiencing at least one armed conflict during the period 1992-2001

hundreds of miles of sea-grass in the region. Burning oil wells created acid rain and black snow as far away as Kashmir (1,500 miles distant). Unparalleled destruction is the legacy of modern war: toxic munitions, unexploded weapons and the ruin of soil and landscape. Further, war often leads to mass movements of people who are forced to destroy everything in their path as they try to survive. Refugees have no choice but to burn all available wood to cook and boil their water to avoid infection.[11]

And before World War Two, the Japanese were already exploiting natural resources at an unsustainable rate to build up a war chest. During the War 15 per cent of Japan's forests were logged. And in 1945 came the atomic bomb and its destruction of Hiroshima and Nagasaki. Today, any nuclear war would risk creating a two-year nuclear winter with unimaginable human and environmental consequences.[10]

While war creates environmental disaster it is also true that environmental disaster can lead to conflict. Displaced people have few options and issues over access to water will increasingly foment antagonism, as already happens in the Middle East. One bleak view of the future is that for the next century the North, having depleted its own environmental resources, will be increasingly driven to military intervention in the South to secure continuing access to their as-yet undepleted resources. Thus the North/South relationship will have moved full circle from colonialism to 'development' to the North's control of risk and security in order to ensure continued access to resources in the former colonies.

Lest we forget...

'War has a look. It is the bloody and anonymous bodies. It is the billowy mushroom cloud, the wall of flame rising from a forest that's been napalmed, the sky of Kuwait blackened by oil fires.' *William Tsutsui*, Japanese-American historian. ■

Genocide such as traumatized Germany, Cambodia, Rwanda or the Sudan is the most extreme form of conflict. Watching the collecting of the skulls which were once mothers, fathers, siblings and children are

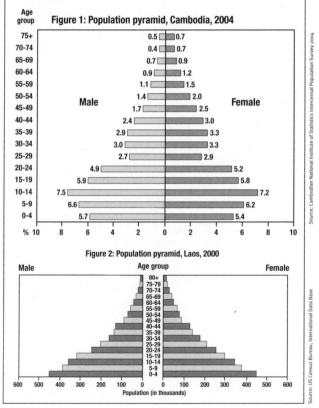

Killing fields

One legacy of Cambodia's bloody past under Pol Pot is the profile of its population today – the pyramid does not rise in neat steps as a result of the 1980s genocide, and because so many died in their twenties there are fewer children born. See the comparable population profile for neighboring Laos, below.

Figure 1: Population pyramid, Cambodia, 2004

Age group	Male	Female
75+	0.5	0.7
70-74	0.4	0.7
65-69	0.7	0.9
60-64	0.9	1.2
55-59	1.1	1.5
50-54	1.4	2.0
45-49	1.7	2.5
40-44	2.4	3.0
35-39	2.9	3.3
30-34	3.0	3.3
25-29	2.7	2.9
20-24	4.9	5.2
15-19	5.9	5.8
10-14	7.5	7.2
5-9	6.6	6.2
0-4	5.7	5.4

% 10 8 6 4 2 0 2 4 6 8 10

Source: Cambodian National Institute of Statistics Intercensal Population Survey 2004

Figure 2: Population pyramid, Laos, 2000

Male   Age group   Female

80+ 75-79 70-74 65-69 60-64 55-59 50-54 45-49 40-44 35-39 30-34 25-29 20-24 15-19 10-14 5-9 0-4

600 500 400 300 200 100 0 0 100 200 300 400 500 600
Population (in thousands)

Source: US Census Bureau, International Data Base

the generations of those left behind to face a world where there is no safety, no security, no human warmth, no rules any more. In 1995, camps for displaced people in Rwanda provided physical security to women who had seen so many deaths, and been raped so repeatedly that, although their bodies had survived, their minds had not. They did not respond to questions and when looking into their eyes there was no-one 'at home' to talk to. Doctors caring for these women's physical needs had come as volunteers from the calm of Australia and Japan; they needed psychological counseling after having had to deal with such evidence of human evil and the despair it caused. Yet even that was not the end, for the camps themselves were often run by gangs who had been part of the killing process. But there were also remarkable signs of hope. Such as the man scavenging for his 'family' of 11 children, none of them biologically related to him, but whom he had gradually gathered as his search for his own 6 children revealed that none had survived. Or the school-teacher who had decided that the one

---

Cambodian vision

'I was 8 years old on 17 April 1975. Two Khmer Rouge soldiers, each holding a gun, told us to evacuate. 'Don't worry, you will be back in three days', they assured us. By 1979, only four other members of my immediate family – my grandmother, my two aunts, and my brother in Paris were still alive. My mother, sister, and other brother had perished of malnutrition, starvation and illness, and my father had been murdered. I am sorry to hear of Im Chan's death. [This sculptor was one of only 7 survivors of the prison Tuol Sleng where 14,000 educated Khmer were tortured to death]. We Khmers are Buddhists and believe in the impermanent nature of things. Therefore, we accept life and death as part of this ephemeral and transient cycle.

[When told no-one cried at the funeral] Perhaps veiled behind those blank eyes are outpourings of tears comparable to the torrential rainstorms that we once experienced in Cambodia.' ■

Boreth Ly in *Art Journal* Spring 2003. The article is illustrated with a photograph of a skull where the blindfold has outlasted the flesh.

---

thing she could do was teach. In a battered tin trunk she collected all the bits of paper, stubs of pencil and random printed pages she could find and was just sitting against the wall of a roofless house teaching a band of small, lost children.[11]

Rising from the chaos

After violent internal conflicts, countries are faced by the 'perfect storm' of post-conflict recovery: few people to work; big debts; disease and poor economic prospects.[12] Many of these countries were very poor even before the conflict, with low literacy and high child and maternal mortality (see table *Conflict costs* on page 123). Sometimes HIV/AIDS was already a severe problem. In these cases, movements by troops, militias and refugees ensure that the disease spreads even when there has not been a campaign of rape to terrorize the civilian population.

Countries with rich natural resources such as diamonds, minerals or timber are particularly vulnerable to war, as Angola, the Congo and Sierra Leone have all discovered to their cost. The UN has worked on a regime for the certification of diamonds so as to effectively put sanctions on dealers in conflict diamonds.[13]

Experts continue to debate the question of whether more civil conflicts are motivated by grievance or greed. Economists feed vast amounts of data into complex models but have no valid information on unemployment and under-employment, which could be the crucial factors fuelling conflict. It may well be that there is no real distinction between greed and grievance. There is little logic in saying that where young men (for it is usually young men) from an ethnic group which feels that it has been discriminated against and denied its share of the national wealth take up arms they are motivated by greed where there are 'lootable' resources (such as Angolan diamonds)

The costs of war

and grievance where there are not (Somalia). As noted earlier, in Sierra Leone young men can feel excluded by a system in which all power and wealth and even wives go to older men.[14] But none of these really explain why men fight so readily.

As we have seen, however poor a country is, war makes it more impoverished. This occurs not just through the destruction of roads, schools, clinics and homes but also through the loss of people – 'human capital' – as those with skills are killed, caught up in the military or flee the country. Most importantly there is impoverishment through the destruction of bonds between people and their willingness to help each other.

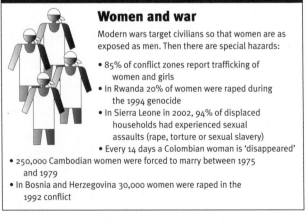

Women and war

Modern wars target civilians so that women are as exposed as men. Then there are special hazards:

- 85% of conflict zones report trafficking of women and girls
- In Rwanda 20% of women were raped during the 1994 genocide
- In Sierra Leone in 2002, 94% of displaced households had experienced sexual assaults (rape, torture or sexual slavery)
- Every 14 days a Colombian woman is 'disappeared'
- 250,000 Cambodian women were forced to marry between 1975 and 1979
- In Bosnia and Herzegovina 30,000 women were raped in the 1992 conflict

Source: *Stop Violence against Women* (Amnesty International 2004)

War creates widows and widowers. Widowers can usually remarry because of the overall shortage of men and 'surplus' of women. Widows are disadvantaged both by having to do so many things alone and by the fact that many cultures actively discriminate against them. Life is, of course, even harder for widows who have been raped in the war and find themselves pregnant. In the aftermath of any violent conflict it is important to look out for the fate of pregnant widows – a group of no concern to most political leaders and neglected even by well-meaning mediators.[15]

Child soldiers

One of the most tragic costs of war is the creation of child soldiers: young boys and girls who never get to be children and have their adult lives damned in advance. In *The Brothers Karamazov*, Dostoyevsky argued that every death of an innocent child questions the existence of God – yet there are religious groups around the world who argue that the recruitment of

---

Children in arms

There are some 300,000 child soldiers; about one-third are girls.

- The average recruitment age was 13 – the youngest started fighting aged seven.
- 58 per cent of the children said that they had joined up 'voluntarily'; only 23 per cent reported physical coercion.
- Many children fleeing hunger, physical and/or sexual abuse or collapse of their community spoke of finding refuge and support in armed groups.
- The majority of situations where children were recruited as soldiers are conflicts associated with ethnic or religious differences.
- Social and cultural pressures, and family expectations, often drive children to take up arms in defense of a way of life perceived as under attack.
- Parents or leaders often 'volunteer' children to serve in armed groups, especially where conflicts span generations and are based on an ethnic minority's struggle for survival. ∎

Source: UNICEF *Adult Wars, Child Soldiers: Voices of children involved in Conflict in the East Asia and Pacific Region, 2001.*

---

child soldiers even by force is justifiable.

After the fighting stops, child soldiers are left to face the continuing nightmares; the difficulty of controlling anger; alcohol and drug addiction; inability to concentrate on learning tasks and loathing self-hatred. These are the unseen costs of war.

Disability

Another tragic cost of warfare is the vast numbers of people, adults and children alike, who are maimed and left with one or more missing limbs. In some cases this is the result of landmines and unexploded ordinance of all kinds which have randomly blighted the lives of those who found themselves in the wrong place. Peasant farmers often face the choice between cultivating fields still sprinkled with landmines or starving. You might ponder this as you stand in the supermarket aisle choosing your breakfast cereal.

In other cases, the maiming has been a part of a deliberate strategy of fighting in which cutting off the hand of one's enemy is preferable to killing her/him because it creates more terror and a one-handed person still has to be fed where a corpse does not. Such extreme violence is deliberately intended to prevent reconciliation, to ensure that there is no going back to an earlier state of affairs where people lived and worked together irrespective of their ethnic or national origins. To think of maiming adults and

---

'We were drugged and ordered to move forwards on the battlefield. We did not know what sort of drug or alcohol we were given but we drank it because we were very tired, very thirsty and hungry. We had walked for two whole days under very hot burning sun. The hill (battlefield) had no shade, trees were burnt and artillery shells were exploding everywhere. We were so scared, very thirsty and some of us collapsed due to over-tiredness. But we were beaten from behind (by the officers) and had to move forward. One got killed.' *Myo Win*, a 14-year-old Burmese. Source: BBC World Service, 'Children of Conflict'. ■

forcing children to become killers as a part of a deliberate strategy of civil warfare, is to begin to understand just how difficult resolution will be. Is it easier to forgive the man who killed your mother or those who incited a child to hack off her foot or a youth to rape her?

War destroys economies

Beyond the dead bodies, and the people with missing limbs begging in the streets, the most obvious costs of civil conflict are in the destruction of national economies and their physical infrastructure – the sheer financial costs of paying for the fighting and the reconstruction after the event. In the case of the DRC (formerly Zaire) the World Bank approach for 2003 was to 'reduce tensions' with a $164 million grant and a $50 million loan. This represents a little over $200 million to restore order in a country which has experienced some five million conflict-induced deaths in the previous five years: that's $40 per death. Before the onset of civil war in 1996, Mobutu's Zaire was arguably the most corrupt country in the world. In those days the US was happy to pay Mobutu personally to keep Zaire on the 'right' side in the Cold War

---

Landmine peril

Around the world more than 1,000 people per month are killed by landmines. In Cambodia one in every 236 people is a landmine amputee: in Angola one in 470 and in northern Somalia one in 1,000. These entire societies are affected by the insidious presence of the mines. The International Committee of the Red Cross found that of those who survive, only one in four of those injured get medical care within six hours, one in six has to travel for more than three days to get treatment. The wounds usually require at least two operations to treat. Growing children face exceptional difficulties; they need multiple operations and new prosthesis every six months. A child injured now is going to need 20 prostheses over a lifetime at a cost of $3,000: this in countries where the annual income is just $300. Most jobs available in these countries require physical fitness which rules out amputees. ■

as well as paying an extra 'local allowance' to all US Government officials so that they could cover the bribes demanded with every transaction (to cash a traveler's check; to enter the auction for seats on weekly plane flights to and from the regions). The war has destroyed relatively little infrastructure because there was little to destroy.

The 'Peace Dividend'

The converse of the huge costs of war is the reality that preparing for peace brings a 'peace dividend'. It is sometimes argued, especially by right-wingers and arms manufacturers, that military expenditure is good for the economy. This is rather like arguing that a boy who throws a rock through a window is good for the economy because a glazier needs to be employed to mend the window. The fallacy lies in not asking what the money could or would have been spent on instead. From those who could think of better ways of spending the money, there were great expectations of a general peace dividend after the fall of the Berlin Wall

---

The sheer waste

- The total economic cost of Sri Lanka's war between 1983 and 1996 was about $4.20 billion – double its 1996 Gross Domestic Product (GDP).
- Per capita GDP in the Basque region of Spain declined by about 10 per cent, compared with a region without any such violence, with the difference in per capita GDP widening in response to spikes in terrorist activity.
- The economies of Greece, Israel, and Turkey were adversely affected by terrorist incidents, and their market shares of tourist trade also fell, with spill over effects for other Mediterranean countries.
- Tighter security precautions put in place in the wake of the terrorist attacks of 11 September 2001, have been estimated to cost the world about $75 billion.
- The IMF's World Economic Outlook, December 2001: The Global Economy After September 11 indicated that the long-term cost could be as high as 0.75 per cent of world GDP.[16] ∎

---

and the end of the Cold War. Then came the 'War on Terror' and the creation of 'coalitions of the willing' and cynicism returned. Yet, for a time there was a real post-Cold War peace dividend.

An IMF study in 1991 found that world military spending declined by 1.3 percentage points of GDP between 1985 and 1990, with declines in all regions and for both industrial and developing countries. More recent data for the 130 IMF member countries show that worldwide military spending declined from 3.6 per cent of world production in 1990 to 2.4 per cent in 1995, with most of the savings taking place in the transition economies and the industrial countries. The reduction was widespread; 90 of the 130 countries reduced the proportion of military outlays during the period, while only 40 maintained or increased them.[17]

With a peace dividend, governments can then choose to spend the money which they would otherwise have spent on the military or importing arms, on education, health or civil infrastructure. Yet the military are very powerful in many developing countries (and in the North) and they can use their political clout and even the threat of insurrection to block cuts to military spending. Often the military is the largest single government bureaucracy. It produces nothing. It just consumes taxpayers' money. This goes to making small arms or weapons of mass destruction and to those who operate them. The military do not create wealth. They divert it from more productive uses. The reason why the countries of Europe took centuries to become developed countries was that any progress made in any given century tended to be wiped out by the impact of repeated wars.

According to SIPRI (the Stockholm Peace Research Institute), global military spending in 2004 broke the $1 trillion barrier for the first time since the Cold War, boosted by the 'war on terror' and the growing defense budgets of India and China. The US spends more than $400 billion a year on its military. Russia, the next largest spender, spends only 14 per cent as much. To equal US spending the military budgets of the next 27 highest spenders have to be added together. This fact together with the US nuclear stockpile and the 120 countries where the US has troops shows why so many regard the US as an imperialist power and a threat to peace, In Iraq the war has cost twice the annual GDP of the country – that is, the US has spent $2 on destruction for every $1 which is created.

Bread not guns

Estimates are that the Iraq War and subsequent reconstruction may cost $600 billion, yet for a mere $24 billion it would be possible to ensure that no-one goes hungry. In other words, for just four per cent of the cost of that war we could feed the world. There are currently some 840 million who go to bed hungry each night who could be saved by this humble sum.

Globally, there is a chain of causation in which development brings peace, forgiveness heals societies and justice and peace belong together. There is also a long-standing agreed UN target for developed countries to spend just 0.7 per cent of their national product on international aid. Only the Dutch and the Scandinavians meet even this modest target. The US spends 0.1 per cent and the UK 0.33 per cent. Yet adding just 1.5 pence or 3 cents to the basic tax rate could raise the UK to the target. Alternatively, abolishing direct agricultural subsidies in the UK could pay for this, as could a reduction of just 12 per cent in the national defense budget. It is not customary for government finance ministers to compare the amounts they spend on defense/war with the amounts they spend on international aid/peace yet

Conflict costs

War-torn countries suffer not just from the loss of lives, but also the long-term effects of displacement and disruption as well as from the effects of ruined economies and infrastructures.

Where	Years of conflict	Civilian deaths	Debt per person	Child mortality rate	% displaced	Refugees	Population at end 2003	HDI rank*
Afghanistan	24	1,000,000	$84	257	5	500,000	28,700,000	N/A
Angola	36	1,500,000	$756	260	18	300,000	12,700,000	164
Burundi	10	300,000	$180	190	18	450,000	6,100,000	171
Cambodia	30	1,850,000	$229	138	6	700,000	11,800,000	130
Chechnya	10	118,000	-	N/A	29	10,000	800,000	-
DR Congo	5	5,000,000	$201	205	6	410,000	56,600,000	167
Guatemala	36	200,000	$455	58	11	200,000	11,000,000	119
Liberia	14	250,000	$606	235	19	120,000	3,300,000	N/A
Nepal	6	10,000	$107	91	1	20,000	25,300,000	143
Rwanda	1	800,000	$140	183	1	65,000	9,300,000	158
Sierra Leone	11	200,000	$214	316	7	35,000	5,600,000	177
Somalia	13	500,000	$312	225	11	300,000	8,000,000	N/A
Sri Lanka	19	163,000	$440	19	3	155,000	19,300,000	99
Sudan	35	2,000,000	$525	107	14	500,000	38,100,000	138
Total*	**289**	**14,061,000**	-	-	-	**4,000,000**	**247,000,000**	-
Average	18.1	937,400	$554	165	11	-	-	141

*Total also includes Haiti and Lebanon.

*HDI = The UN's Human Development Index. The index ranks countries in terms of life expectancy, educational attainment and adjusted real income. Sierra Leone is currently ranked lowest (177), while Norway is ranked first.

Source: Based on World Vision, *An Ounce of Prevention: the Failure of G8 Policy on Armed Conflict, 2004*: Annex A; *Human Development Report 2004*, UNDP.

this is a rational calculus. Currently, for every pound the UK Government spends on aid, it spends nine on the military. The campaign to Make Poverty History and the Live 8 concert pushed these issues to the fore at the time of the 2005 meeting of the G8 richest countries in Scotland.

Countries without armies

At the other extreme to countries facing the costs of mass civil bloodshed are those brave countries which are so peaceful that they do not have armies at all. There are currently 28 such countries. They are Andorra, Cook Islands, Costa Rica, Dominica, Micronesia, Gambia, Grenada, Haiti, Iceland, Kiribati, Liechtenstein, Maldives, Marshall Islands, Mauritius, Monaco, Niue, Northern Marianas, Palau, Panama, St Kitts and Nevis, St Lucia, St Vincent and the Grenadines, Samoa, San Marino, Solomon Islands, Tuvalu, Vanuatu, and Vatican City.[18] Some have defense arrangements with another country.

There would have been more countries without military forces but the departing colonial powers

---

Rich coast, no army

Costa Rica is the only Central American country with a long-standing democratic tradition and, not coincidentally, the only one without an army. It has been an oasis of relative peace and prosperity in a region sadly known for repression and misery. Its army was abolished in 1949 after a year of military rule.

Yet there is now a war of words between the right-wing establishment that controls the media, and a growing collection of former presidents and concerned citizens who fear that the media are trying to redesign the country's social traditions. In particular, the media are attacking Costa Rica's lack of an army, its tradition of neutrality, and its tolerance of domestic leftists.

The message from the media is that Costa Rica must change its ways and raise an army or be overrun by its neighbor to the north, Nicaragua. See more on Costa Rica's vision in box A world without armies, chapter 7. ■

wanted to leave them with armies, modeled after their own, which would continue to co-operate with the home country in any regional disputes and, even more importantly, would continue to purchase arms from their former rulers. Examples of the two-facedness of ex-colonial arms links are too common to excite comment. Just one example will suffice: at the same time that the UK was reading Tanzania lectures on cutting back expenditure and not being able to afford universal primary education, the UK Government pushed through the sale of a $53 million military air traffic control system which Tanzania was trying to avoid and which even the World Bank labeled as a waste of money. In 2001 the UK Government granted export licenses to cover arms sales to 31 out of the 41 poorest countries in the world. Hot spots cheerfully supplied included Colombia, Sri Lanka, Algeria and Zimbabwe. If the UK were to give up all arms exports this would have a one-off effect, only reducing the national product by 0.4 per cent; thus the Government's support to the arms industry, if rational, must be based on security rather than economic considerations.[19]

Future hope

Just as war and civil violence bring great costs, so peace can bring great benefits where there is the will to work together. The next chapter looks at some of the ways forward.

The costs of war

1 See www.ministryforpeace.org.uk 2 www.guerillalaw.com/mediation.html
3 R Rummel *Death by Government* (Transaction 1994). 4 On 28/10/2004
The Lancet released a report on post-war deaths in Iraq; the ensuing
debate on the web shows the complexity of these issues. 5 G Harris 'The
costs of armed conflict' in G. Harris editor *Recovery from Armed Conflict
in Developed Countries* (Routledge 1999). 6 P Wrobel *Disarmament and
Conflict Resolution: Nicaragua and El Salvador* (United Nations 1997), p 125.
7 F Stewart 'War and underdevelopment: can economic analysis help reduce
the costs', *Journal of International Development*, 5(4), 357-80, 1993. 8 See S
Dolittle 'Ten reasons why militarism is bad for the environment' www.umass.
edu/peri/warandpeace.html 9 See 'The environmental impacts of war' www.
islandpress.org/eco-compass/war 10 P Rogers 'The environmental costs of
war' www.preparingforpeace.org 11 H Ware *Field Notes*, Kigali, 1995. 12 World
Vision *An Ounce of Prevention: The Failure of G8 Policy on Armed Conflict*,
2004. 13 www.diamonds.net maintains an information service on combating
conflict diamonds. 14 P Richards *Fighting for the Rain Forest: War, Youth and
Resources in Sierra Leone*, 1996. 15 For the situation of stigma and harassment in Sri Lanka see http://www.peacewomen.org/news/SriLanka/Novo3/
woes.htm 16 www.imf.org/external/pubs/ft/fandd/2002/12/gupta.htm 17 B
Clements, S Gupta and J Schiff *'What happened to the peace dividend?'* (World
Bank 2002). 18 See The UN Commission on Human Rights and the website
Demilitarization.com 19 See www.saferworld.org.uk

7 Imagine living life in peace

*'I think this cruelty will end and that peace and
tranquility will return again.'*
Anne Frank (1929-1945),
victim of Nazi persecution.

**This chapter focuses on building lasting peace, as in
Gandhi's constructive program of domestic and social
progress to create positive peace. Peace and justice
are two sides of the same coin.**

THERE IS A Zen story about a man on a galloping
horse who is asked where he is going. He shouts
back 'I don't know, ask the horse'. This is the fate of
those who make peace by force but, as in Iraq, have
no clear vision of how they are going to re-build
a peaceful society. Before setting out on the road
to peace it is important to figure out how we will
know when we have reached that point. Yes, the
guns will have stopped firing and the machetes will
be restricted to the fields again, but what else can
we foresee? We may only be able to move gradually,
even two steps forward and one step back, towards
our goals, but we need to know what our goals are
and how to measure their attainment. Obviously,
elements such as human rights for all are non-nego-
tiable: everyone should have the right to practice
their religion; speak their mind and their own
language and practice their culture so long as this
does not harm anyone else or interfere with other
people's freedom. But that, as we have seen, may
not be straightforward at all.

People's material wellbeing can be even more difficult to achieve because this requires sharing of
resources, and making everyone happy is harder to
achieve. Progressive tax systems can greatly help poor
people but at the cost of some loss of wealth to the

Evolving peace

'What's odd is that when you try to think about peace, you end up mostly thinking about war... but surely peace is something more than the mere absence of something else... Peace is not the rarefied and unblemished state of our fondest imaginings, but a more common experience that includes conflict but is not consumed by it. Peace is not a fixed or final state of being but an experimental and evolving process, necessarily imperfect and always tending towards a harmony that may never be fully attained.' Mark Sommer in *Whole Earth Review*, Summer 1986. ∎

---

rich. Hoping that rich people will agree to more taxes out of altruism and recognition of human interdependence – or at the very least because they recognize that redistribution improves their own security – may be pie in the sky. Certainly, the Tobin Tax on currency speculation could help offset imbalances.

'Structural violence' occurs where a group of people, often defined by their race, ethnicity, caste and/or religion are systematically denied their rights – for example where some groups have to watch their children starving whilst others in the same society are growing fat or throwing food away.

With the political will, it is easy to legislate to allow freedom of religion or of speech for all; it is a much more demanding goal to try to legislate for enough food for everyone. In an ideal world, no-one would be imprisoned for stealing food to feed hungry children nor would anyone need to steal to feed their children. To quote a Latin American peasant: 'I am for peace, but not peace with hunger.'[1]

Mark Sommer (see box) has an action plan for a peace system based on allowing the military only defensive weapons; training civilians in non-violent defense; political integration to handle each issue at the most local level practicable; conversion of military manufacturing to produce social goods ('swords to ploughshares') and cultural adaptation to accept differences of view but a commonality of fates.

Safety catches on

Even with their safety catches on, guns raise questions about the form of peace- building in mind. Is there to be the US practice with everyone having their own gun or the Solomon Islands' model where only the police may have guns and these are kept locked up?[2] Is there to be a standing army, even when the evidence suggests that armies cause wars, as their expense has to be justified and the troops kept occupied? Should the government spend its money on buying weapons or on providing education and health services for its poorer citizens? Do those who are providing aid to poor countries have the right or responsibility to

---

A world without armies

Following a civil war that killed 2,000 people, Costa Rica's then victorious leader José Figueres made a revolutionary pronouncement on 1 December 1948: 'The Regular Army of Costa Rica today gives the key to its military base to the schools… [T]he Government hereby declares the National Army officially abolished.' As a result the nation's limited resources were channelled into infrastructure, especially education and health, which rewarded the country with the highest living standard in Central and South America. Nobel Peace Prize winner and former President, Oscar Arias Sánchez, reflects:

'The abolition of the army helped us avoid the quagmire that in the following decades would slowly engulf our neighbors: deepening poverty, brutal military repression, guerrilla movements and foreign military intervention. If Costa Rica had an army in the 1980s, we almost certainly would have become like Honduras – a militarized outpost of the US in its campaign against the Nicaraguan Government. Instead we were able to promote a regional peace plan, to keep our economy growing and to build new schools.'

Fourteen countries have now followed Costa Rica's example and demilitarized through Constitutional amendments. Twenty-eight nations now have no armies. Dr Arias encouraged and supported the Presidents of two of these countries – Panama and Haiti – to demilitarize. 'My goal was to impress on them the importance of preventing the rule of men with guns. Abolishing the army reduces the immediate threat of coups, but without a comprehensive program to disarm and reintegrate soldiers into society, armed groups can reform under a different banner.' ∎

Source: From an interview by Chris Richards, *New Internationalist*, 381, August 2005.

require a reduction in military expenditures? What happened in Costa Rica when it abolished its army (see box p 129) has some of the answers.

Equality and equity

In Martin Luther King's words, 'True peace is more than the absence of war, it is the presence of justice.' Justice, necessary to create positive peace, requires that everyone should have their basic needs met. Currently, one person in four lives in brutal poverty without the bare essentials of life. Children still starve, yet the world has the wealth and the technology to feed everyone adequately. What is lacking is the political will to prevent starvation. One of the many evils of the division of the world into sovereign states is that active compassion tends to stop at national borders. Democracies normally do not let their own citizens starve but their concerns do not always extend to other nations[3] – although there are examples of poor countries such as Malawi who have hosted refugee populations for years. Meanwhile, President Mugabe of Zimbabwe has given a new twist to the link between democracy and hunger by refusing to let food aid reach his political opponents on the eve of an election: 'Vote for me or watch your children starve.'

A future without violence

The goal of peace building is a future without violence; a future where differences and conflict exist but are settled without recourse to weaponry or bloodshed. Sound impossible? Think again. The world has already witnessed many examples of repressive regimes being overthrown with a minimum of violence. How has this happened? Certainly politicians, diplomats and mediators have facilitated the process but most of the work was done by ordinary people like you and me using nonviolent resistance. Only a relatively small percentage of these stories are ever properly documented and even fewer are publicized. After all, when was the last time you read a news item about the quiet diplomacy or nonviolent action that averted war? Even well documented events such as the 'people power' revolution that ousted the Marcos regime in the Philippines are quickly forgotten, consigned to history's dusty bookshelves. Sadly, *learning* from these stories is something that we appear to be either unwilling or unable to do. This, of course, is in stark contrast to the failures of diplomacy, of conflict prevention, or the so-called 'successes' of military intervention, of which we are constantly reminded, usually in order to justify further military intervention.

Philippines solution

President Ferdinand Marcos in the Philippines commanded 153,000 troops but was toppled in 1986 by nonviolent protest. One of the reasons for the lack of interest in applying the lessons learnt from successful nonviolence is that many of the most dramatic stories seem too difficult to replicate. Yet the sequence of events (see below) that brought an end to Marcos' corrupt rule yields a wealth of insights to be applied elsewhere.

One example is the role that the media played, especially Radio Veritas, the 'friendly' radio station that broadcast messages appealing for people to support the rebels. Then there were the strikes, boycotts and acts of mass civil disobedience that brought the country to a halt.

Toppling Milosevic

These same tactics were used with great effect in Serbia, starting with the coalminers' strike at Kolubara, which followed the rigged election in 2000. It eventually led to a massive coordinated nonviolent uprising in Belgrade which toppled the Milosevic regime that same year. Nothing could stop the sea of people. There too, as in the streets of Manila, police were both without a viable strategy and unwilling to act against the people. 'We had secret talks with the army and the police,' said one of the opposition leaders in the run-up to the Serbian revolution, 'and the deal was that they would not disobey, but neither would they execute. If they had said no, other units would have been brought in. So they said yes when Milosevic asked for action – and they did nothing.'

Nonviolence wins

Of course, what unites these two remarkable stories is the use of peaceful action as a strategic weapon. In both cases, the opposition could have used violence but chose not to. Indeed one of the most successful opposition movements in Serbia, Otpor 'resistance', had a very clear policy of nonviolence.[4] They were well aware that had they fought Milosevic's more powerful

Argentina's Mothers of the Disappeared

At the end of April 1977 a group of 14 women gathered in the Plaza de Mayo in the heart of Buenos Aires. They were there to seek an audience with the Minister of the Interior to discover what had happened to their sons and daughters who had disappeared under the brutal junta regime ruling Argentina. When they first gathered, no-one gave them support. Few people dared even acknowledge that young people were disappearing; that children were being taken in the streets, from their homes, in front of their parents, from their offices, walking home from the university.

Most of the 'disappeared' were never to be heard from again. After imprisonment and torture they were shot, they were beaten to death, even thrown live from airplanes over the sea. This was the most vicious period of the Dirty War between 1976 and 1979 when 30,000 people 'disappeared'. The military dictatorship declared these young people 'subversives', enemies of the State. Their crimes had been to care for the poor, to attend a meeting against the Government, to be a sister, brother or friend of someone who attended such a meeting.

The women identified each other by the scarves they wore – made from cloth diapers, usually from their own children, and saved for their grandchildren who would now never be. Their desperation gave them strength. They began to gather on park benches in front of the Congressional House. They took out a one-page advertisement in the national press demanding to know where their children were and sent

henchmen, it would have only strengthened his hand, giving him greater powers to suppress dissenters.

In the Philippines, the conspirators had initially planned to attack the palace, either capturing or killing Marcos. However the plan was leaked to the President and a trap had been laid, with thousands of marines lying in waiting ready for a counter-offensive. Had the rebels carried out their plan, they would have been massacred. Marcos might well have persuaded himself, his people and the international community that such bloodshed and even further repression was justified on the grounds that an armed rebellion had been launched against him. Even if the conspirators' plan had not been discovered, and they had succeeded in killing Marcos, would a violent coup have won over the rest of the armed forces, many of whom were fiercely loyal to the regime? Would a coup have been welcomed by

---

petitions signed by tens of thousands to the President. They garnered global media attention in 1978 when soccer's World Cup was played in Argentina. When the military regime finally fell, they continued to struggle against the democratically elected government which was all for wiping the slate clean and granting amnesty to all the human rights abusers during the Dirty War. The mothers established a genetic data bank to determine the identity of bodies discovered. Their remaining sons and daughters have now taken up their struggle, and have formed an organization called HIJOS (Children for Identity and Justice and against Forgetting and Silence).

The mothers still walk in the Plaza de Mayo every Thursday. In the middle of the Plaza, a white ceramic circle around the Pyramid of Liberty Monument shows the path of their journey begun 30 years ago. Embedded also are symbols of the white scarves they wear, embroidered in blue cross-stitch with the names of their disappeared children. Now their path is memorialized, and people walk with them, honored to be in their presence. Nominated for the Nobel Peace Prize, the Mothers of the Plaza de Mayo have become an icon of women's resistance against tyranny; supporting each other 'in circle'. The depths inside the eyes of those still walking in the Plaza de Mayo show a lesson in pain suffered, pain remembered, and pain overcome.

Source: www.peacexpeace.org/peacepapers/plazademayo.html

the people? Would the international community have accepted as legitimate a regime that took power by force, even if launched in support of the democratically elected opposition leader? Ultimately, partly through circumstance and partly by design, the use of non-violent action was a strategic trump card which wrong-footed the regime and led to its downfall. Faced by hundreds of thousands of demonstrators: men, women, children, priests, nuns, urban rebels with linked arms blocking troop movements, President Marcos, finally abandoned by the US, realized that his troops would not obey any command to fire on civilians who were demonstrating peacefully.

Vichy France

Such stories are not as rare as one may think. In Vichy France, one small community resisted all attempts by the Nazis to deport the Jews seeking refuge in the village. The military commander of the region, Major Schmehling, explained to the Gestapo chief, Colonel Metzger, why it was useless to fight the villagers: 'I told Metzger that this kind of resistance had nothing to do with violence, nothing to do with anything we could destroy with violence.'

198 ways to leave the violence

Peaceful resistance to oppression is only one way to end conflict. In *The Politics of Nonviolent Action* Gene Sharp lists 198 different tools available to the nonviolent activist, giving real-life examples of where they have worked. The peaceful revolutionar-ies in Serbia used Sharp's book to create their own Serbian language manual. To Sharp's list can be added hundreds of techniques that have been used by people not only to help prevent, contain or end bloodshed but also to encourage, consolidate and build a sustain-able peace. While not as dramatic as the Philippine people power revolution, the impact of many of these

Another brick in the wall

Below are some ideas and actions people can take in their own lives to help promote a more peaceful world.

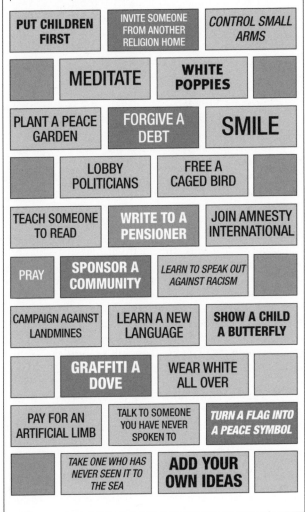

PUT CHILDREN FIRST	INVITE SOMEONE FROM ANOTHER RELIGION HOME	CONTROL SMALL ARMS

MEDITATE — WHITE POPPIES

PLANT A PEACE GARDEN — FORGIVE A DEBT — SMILE

LOBBY POLITICIANS — FREE A CAGED BIRD

TEACH SOMEONE TO READ — WRITE TO A PENSIONER — JOIN AMNESTY INTERNATIONAL

PRAY — SPONSOR A COMMUNITY — LEARN TO SPEAK OUT AGAINST RACISM

CAMPAIGN AGAINST LANDMINES — LEARN A NEW LANGUAGE — SHOW A CHILD A BUTTERFLY

GRAFFITI A DOVE — WEAR WHITE ALL OVER

PAY FOR AN ARTIFICIAL LIMB — TALK TO SOMEONE YOU HAVE NEVER SPOKEN TO — TURN A FLAG INTO A PEACE SYMBOL

TAKE ONE WHO HAS NEVER SEEN IT TO THE SEA — ADD YOUR OWN IDEAS

interventions is no less remarkable. For example, two of the most devastating civil wars of the 20th century – Mozambique and Guatemala – were both concluded through mediation spearheaded not by government representatives but by ordinary people. What these stories tell us is that people can make a difference – that peacemaking cannot and should not just be left to governments and the professionals. There are many things we can all do to promote peace.

Creating space for peace

Including nonviolent elements into all aspects of peace-making and peacekeeping is essential to transform the way we manage conflict. Unless the reality of exploitation built into global power structures and shown at local levels is directly addressed, there will be no space for values essential for sustainable recovery. Current peace-building practice fails to address the structural causes of conflict and is set up following adversarial negotiations and policed by peacekeepers. Whilst the peacekeepers can secure a pause in the shooting, fighting will soon start again unless the social and economic causes of the dispute are dealt with. People from all groups need to start working together to meet their needs as they define them. Nurturing and supporting their skills in peaceful ways to end discord is also important. Unless this happens, the peace initiatives in Iraq, Afghanistan and the Solomons risk sowing the seeds of further violence. Democracy and civic participation are cultural patterns which need time to develop.

We use the term 'nonviolence' because it is widely known and understood but its negativity is unfortunate: rather like calling light 'non-darkness'. So stuck

---

'A treaty of peace makes, it may be, an end to the war of the moment, but not to the conditions of war which at any time may afford a new pretext for opening hostilities.' *Immanuel Kant* (1724-1804), philosopher. ∎

Paths to peace

There are steps we can all take towards working for nonviolence and peace.

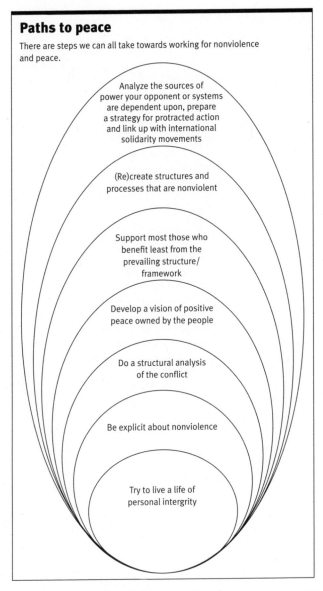

Analyze the sources of power your opponent or systems are dependent upon, prepare a strategy for protracted action and link up with international solidarity movements

(Re)create structures and processes that are nonviolent

Support most those who benefit least from the prevailing structure/ framework

Develop a vision of positive peace owned by the people

Do a structural analysis of the conflict

Be explicit about nonviolence

Try to live a life of personal intergrity

with that phrase, what are the possibilities for integrating nonviolence into peace practice?

We need to keep in mind a far more positive image full of life and joy – see *Paths to Peace* graphic.

Peace needs hard work. Those who seek to end conflict need to understand how social and economic factors cause it and how these can be transformed. This involves discussing with local communities how the global economic system affects them, and how the recovering country is going to position itself in relation to that system. Timor Leste/East Timor, the world's newest nation, is currently battling for more equal rights to its own natural resources of oil and gas. If the present treaty cannot be re-negotiated, the revenue from these resources will not flow through to the new government, and the nation will be left to continued poverty. Analyzing the root causes of the conflict can demonstrate how military power is used to protect the interests of élites (as in Indonesia), and how relations such as those of gender, limit people's potential to participate in building a culture of peace. The outcome of such an analysis could be the development of a vision of positive peace owned by the war-torn communities.

'Above us only sky'

Space needs to be made for people to dream again. 'Imagine all the people living life in peace...' was former Beatle John Lennon's vision. Depending on what local people want, a vision of positive peace could include a commitment to building appropriately democratic patterns, self-reliant local economies and the means for implementing peaceful practices at each level of society.

Such a vision supports those who gain the least from existing economic structures: women, the urban working class and the underclass excluded from the formal economy, the landless, the rural poor and indigenous peoples. When decisions are being made about the future everyone needs to have a say and be involved, not just those with powerful voices. One of the hardest things about this however is that some people (particularly women) do not have time for the endless meetings and talking that democracy requires. Women are powerful agents of peace-building. Actions by Women for Peace in the Solomon Islands, and Bougainville Women for Peace and Freedom both demonstrate how women can promote peace even where violence is spreading out of control like a bush fire. In these matrilineal societies, women have developed the power to create peace-building strategies that affect everyone. They are running trauma-healing workshops both for ex-fighters and their victims and relatives. They are rebuilding the education system and including teaching skills to resolve differences. They are debating the new constitution and are leaders in reconciliation and justice seeking.[5]

As seen, creating a vision of peace has to be both explicitly nonviolent and also address the causes of violence in a systematic way. This involves changing the deep-seated militarism of many societies, and many forms of peacekeeping, which would be better described as peace enforcement.

Encouraging intervention by organizations such as Witnesses for Peace and Peace Brigades International (PBI)[6] can create neutral spaces for communities to begin the peace process. PBI is an NGO that promotes human rights and peaceful transformation of conflicts. Upon invitation they send teams of volunteers into areas of repression and conflict. The volunteers accompany human rights' defenders and others who are threatened by political violence. The theory, which has been validated by experience in Latin America and Asia, is that even government-sponsored thugs behave better in the presence of foreign observers. Action can also involve supporting and promoting self-managed local models of governance and self-reliance, such as the use of renewable energy. For example, the experience of the 9-year communication and economic embargo on Bougainville meant that communities devised their own ways to survive. They designed micro hydroelectric schemes to power their villages, built and maintained village schools, trained teachers and nurses, and even found a coconut oil alternative to diesel which fueled transport and electricity generation.

Finally, it is important to recognize that creating peace starts with the self. In this way, it helps if those who research and practice peace live a life of personal integrity. The most powerful method that external workers in conflict and post-conflict situations can employ is to demonstrate the values, attitudes and behaviors necessary to transform the conflict, while being culturally sensitive. This can mean living simply, supporting local initiatives, finding peaceful solutions to disagreements, respecting the needs and views of all parties, listening compassionately and building close relationships with local people from all sides of the conflict.

> 'The war was like a university. It made us creative, we thought for ourselves, and we discovered alternative ways to survive... We looked at our dependency on outside support. Now we see we must initiate community-based development.' Bougainville Women for Peace and Freedom. ∎

Because structures of violence are entrenched in the international system, peace-building needs to be seen in the context of a long international struggle to build a peaceful, just and sustainable world. Africa, for example, is the continent most torn apart by violence, and the most poor. This came about not from any African default but rather because Africa is the continent which has been the most exploited from outside with the least given in return. Slavery casts a long shadow.

> 'If you want to make peace with your enemy, you have to work with your enemy. Then he becomes your partner.' *Nelson Mandela* (1918-), former South African President. ∎

Conclusion

The strategies suggested here are just some of the possible ways to make sure that the period after a conflict leads on to genuine peace rather than just acting as a lull before the next outbreak of violence. Each method cannot work alone but only as part of a concentric whole. The interweaving of principled and revolutionary nonviolent philosophy and practice into the theories and strategies for building peace and transforming conflict offers new hope for communities suffering the devastation of protracted violence. An explicit commitment to nonviolence will ensure that peace-building strategies will actively work to dismantle structural violence; will transform the potential for future conflict and will create a culture of peace in the longer-term. Peace does not mean to be in a place where there is no noise, trouble or hard work. It means to be able to be in the middle of all of these things and still be calm in your heart because you are working to help others.

> 'Another world is not only possible, she is on her way.' *Arundhati Roy* (1961-), Indian writer and activist. ∎

1 *Voices of the Poor* (World Bank 2000), a study based on interviews with poor people in 60 countries. **2** In the Solomon Islands anyone found with a gun can be imprisoned. **3** A Sen *Development as Freedom* (Anchor 1999). **4** See P Ackerman and J DuVall *A Force More Powerful* (Palgrave 2001). **5** M Havini 'The role of Bougainvillean women in the war and the peace process' in G Harris and others *Building Peace in Bougainville* (University of New England Press 1999) and A Pollard 'Resolving conflict in the Solomon Islands: the Women for Peace approach', *Development Bulletin* 53:34-38 (October 2000). **6** M King and F Cavadini *An Evergreen Island* (Frontyard Films 2000).

Contacts

Index

Bold page numbers refer to main subjects of boxed text.

Index